核心力量训练

（汉英对照）

Core Strength Training

（Chinese-English Bilingual）

黄迎乒　张振东　主编
Compiled by Huang Yingping & Zhang Zhendong

人民体育出版社
PEOPLE'S SPORTS PUBLISHING HOUSE

图书在版编目（CIP）数据

核心力量训练 ： 汉英对照 / 黄迎乒， 张振东主编
. -- 北京 ： 人民体育出版社， 2024
ISBN 978-7-5009-5503-0

Ⅰ. ①核… Ⅱ. ①黄… ②张… Ⅲ. ①大学生一力量训练一汉、英 Ⅳ. ①G808.14

中国版本图书馆CIP数据核字(2018)第290545号

核心力量训练：汉英对照

黄迎乒　张振东　主编
出版发行：人民体育出版社
印　　装：北京盛通印刷股份有限公司

开本：710×1000　16开本　　印张：12.25　　字数：272千字
版次：2024年10月第1版　　印次：2024年10月第1次印刷
书号：ISBN 978-7-5009-5503-0
定价：62.00元

购买本社图书，如遇有缺损页可与发行与市场营销部联系
联系电话：（010）67151482
社　　址：北京市东城区体育馆路8号（100061）
网　　址：https://books.sports.cn/

编委会名单
List of Editorial Committee

主　编

Editor -in-Chief

黄迎乒　张振东

Huang Yingping & Zhang Zhendong

编　委

Editorial Board Members

赵世鹏　杜松健　张文婧

Zhao Shipeng & Du Songjian & Zhang Wenjing

陈晓莹　王安捷　冯汉哲

Chen Xiaoying & Wang Anjie & Feng Hanzhe

刘清燕　田　昕　韩程爽

Liu Qingyan & Tian Xin & Han Chengshuang

动作模特

Motion Models

陈怡秋　王　贺

Chen Yiqiu & Wang He

英文译者

English Translators

郑　灏　吕　茁　赵玉倩

Zheng Hao & Lyu Zhuo & Zhao Yuqian

郑佩璇　聂世轩

Zheng Peixuan & Nie Shixuan

Foreword
前 言

随着我国素质教育的全面推行与基础教育向素质教育的全面转轨，要求当代大学生德、智、体、美、劳全面发展。一方面，大学体育是学校体育与社会体育的衔接点，是大学生健身意识、终身体育习惯和体育能力形成的关键期，随着校园体育文化的快速发展，学校体育的地位逐渐提高；另一方面，当代大学生身心日趋成熟，思维活跃，认知和判断能力都达到了较高水平，这是他们接受高层次教育与实现人格社会化的最佳时期。

With the comprehensive implementation of quality education in China and the comprehensive transition from basic education to quality education, the requirements for the comprehensive development of contemporary college students' moral, intellectual, physical, aesthetic and labor are more urgent. On the one hand, university sports is the connection point between school sports and social sports, and it is also the key period for the formation of college students' fitness awareness, lifelong sports habits and sports ability. With the rapid development of campus sports culture, the status of school sports has gradually improved. On the other hand, contemporary college students have become more mature in mind and body, active in thinking, and have a high level of cognition and judgment. This is the best period for them to accept high-level education and achieve the socialization of personality.

体育文化素养是在先天遗传素质的基础上，通过后天环境与体育教育的影响形成的，包括体质水平、体育知识、体育意识、体育行为、体育技能、体育个性、体育品德等要素的综合素质与修养。体育文化素养是大学生各种体育精神要素及其品质相结合形成的一种体育素质。提升大学生体育素质，增进大学生健康水平，符合素质教育的时代要求，得到了我国高等教育的广泛认同和重视。

Sports culture accomplishment is influenced by the basis of congenital genetic quality and then formed through the influence of acquired environment and physical education. It includes the comprehensive quality and cultivation of physical fitness, sports knowledge, sports awareness, sports behavior, sports skills, sports personality, sports morality and other factors. Sports culture accomplishment is a kind of sports quality formed by the combination of college students' various sports spirit elements and their qualities. Improving the quality of college students' physical education and developing their health level are in line with the requirements of quality education, and they have been widely recognized and valued by China's higher education.

大学生体育素质主要是依托高校体育教育，在促进大学生的全面发展，传授体育知识和能力，培养体育道德的教育过程中逐渐形成的，是体育锻炼和思维活动相辅相成的教育结果。体育教育是一种区别于大学其他学科的教育方式，在大学生素质教育中起到了提高身体素质与体育技术能力，促进心理健康，传播体育知识与文化的重要作用。

The physical education quality of college students is mainly based on college physical education, which is gradually formed in the process of promoting the all-round development of college students, imparting sports knowledge and ability, and cultivating sports morality. It is the result of combining the physical exercise and thinking activities. Physical education is an educational method different from other disciplines in universities. It plays an important role in improving college students' physical fitness and physical skills, promoting their mental health and disseminating sports knowledge and culture in their quality education.

影响大学生身体素质的基础环节是人体体能中的核心力量。核心力量训练是一种新兴的体能训练方法，近年来成为竞技体育界研究的热点，并且开拓了体能训练方法新的研究领域。核心力量在人类基本生产活动中发力的主要环节及上下肢体协同用力上起着承上启下的枢纽作用。人体所有动作都是由以中心肌群为核心的运动链完成的。在体育运动中，任何运动项目的技术动作都不是依靠单一肌群就能完成的，它必须动员许多肌肉群协调做功，核心肌群在此过程中担负着稳定重心、环节发力、传导力量等作用。

The basic link that affects the physical quality of college students is the core strength of the human body. Core strength training is an emerging physical training method. In recent years, it has become a research hotspot in competitive sports area, and has opened up a new research field of physical training methods. The core strength plays a pivotal role in the main links of human basic production activities and the synergy of upper and lower limbs. All movements of the human body are completed by a kinematic chain with a central myocardial group as the core. In sports, the technical movements of any sport are not based on a single muscle group. It must mobilize many muscle groups to coordinate the work. In this process, the core muscle group plays a role in stabilizing the center of gravity, link force, and conduct strength.

核心力量训练在国内外康复训练领域和体能训练领域成果丰硕。中国备战2008年和2012年奥运会的过程中，核心力量训练相关理论作为奥运会备战科技成果被广泛推广到多支国家队，但是核心力量训练较少被用于普通高校体育教学。普通高校在体育课教学中采用“核心力量训练＋评价量表”模式，能够丰富体育课教学体系，正确评价大学生肌肉状况与核心力量训练效果，促进大学生主动参与体育训练，改善大学生的身体素质和运动能力，为其终身体育打下坚实的基础，增强我国国民体质。

The core strength training has achieved fruitful results in the field of rehabilitation training and physical training at home and abroad. In the process of preparing for the 2008 and 2012 Olympic Games in China, the related theories of core strength training were regarded as scientific and technological achievements of the preparations of Olympics and have been widely promoted to many national teams. However, core strength training is less used in physical education in colleges and universities. Ordinary colleges and universities use the “core area strength exercise + evaluation scale” mode in physical education teaching, which can enrich the physical education teaching system, correctly evaluate the muscle condition and core strength training effect of college students, stimulate college students to actively participate in sports training, and improve the physical quality of college students. And it can lay a solid foundation for their lifelong sports and enhancing physical fitness of our national physique.

全书用150余种训练方法，配300余幅高质量示范图，进行徒手、单一器械、复合器械等动作解析，并详细介绍了“核心力量训练＋评价量表”的使用方法。由浅入深、由易到难递进式总结出不同部位核心区力量的训练方法。

The book uses more than 150 kinds of training methods, with more than 300 high-quality demonstration maps, analyzes the movements of freehand, single instruments, composite instruments, etc., and it introduces the use of the "core area strength training + evaluation scale" in detail. from easy to difficult and summarized the method of the strength of the core areas of different parts.

本书在编写过程中参考和借鉴了大量文献和最新成果，特别是顾德明先生的《运动解剖学图谱》。本书由黄迎乒、张振东两位教授带领赵世鹏、杜松健两位硕士研究生共同完成，参加写作团队成员（排名不分先后）有张文婧、陈晓莹、王安捷、冯汉哲、刘清燕、田昕、韩程爽。全书英文译者为郑灏、吕茁、赵玉倩、郑佩璇、聂世轩，动作模特为陈怡秋、王贺。全书最后由黄迎乒、张振东进行统稿、校对。

This book referred to and drew on a large number of documents and the latest research results in the preparation process, especially the motion anatomy maps of Mr. Gu Deming. The book was jointly completed by two professors, Huang Yingping and Zhang Zhendong, led by two postgraduates, Zhao Shipeng and Du Songjian. The team members who participated in the writing (in no particular order) were: Zhang Wenjing, Chen Xiaoying, Wang Anjie, Feng Hanzhe, Liu Qingyan, Tian Xin, and Han Chengshuang. The English translators of the book include Zheng Hao, Lyu Zhuo, Zhao Yuqian, Zheng Peixuan, Nie Shixuan, and the action models are Chen Yiqiu, Wang He. Finally, the whole book was verified and proofread by Huang Yingping and Zhang Zhendong.

本书把"中英文对照"形式和"核心力量训练＋评价量表"模式的主要创新形式写进教学内容，形成教学体系，试图推广到全国高校，达到共同提高大学生的体育文化素质与核心力量之目的，希望对高校教师和大学生体育教学与运动训练工作能够有所启发。本书在编写过程中，还参考了大量中外学者的优质文献，再次对文献作者表示衷心感谢。鉴于编者水平所限，编书过程中难免存在遗漏与不足，书中若有不妥之处，敬请广大读者批评指正。

In this book, the main innovative forms of the "Chinese-English contrast" form and the "core strength exercise + evaluation scale" model are written into the teaching content and form a teaching system. We try to promote it to the national colleges and universities and to improve the sports culture quality and core strength of all college students. We hope that college teachers and college students can be inspired in physical education and sports training. In the process of writing, we also consulted a large number of high-quality literatures of famous Chinese and foreign scholars, and here we express our heartfelt thanks to the authors of the literature once again. Due to the limitations of the editorial level, there are inevitable omissions and deficiencies in the process of compiling books. If there are any inadequacies in the book, comments and suggestions are most welcome!

编者

Editor

2024 年 6 月

June,2024

Contents
目 录

绪 论

Introduction

随着经济和社会的全面发展、民众生活水平的提升，健康已经成为人类社会共同关注的焦点，成为世界各国追求富强、文明的重要内容。2016 年 3 月 17 日，中共中央发布了《中华人民共和国国民经济和社会发展第十三个五年规划纲要》，提出将健康中国作为国家战略实施，文件中多处提及健康中国和体育的关系。2016 年 10 月，我国颁布了《"健康中国 2030"规划纲要》，第一次把"健康中国"提升为国家战略，明确了建设"健康中国"的思路与任务。在党的十九大报告中也提出"加快推进体育强国建设"，这是第一次在党代会中明确提出建设体育强国，体育强国建设是新时期中国体育发展的主要目标和宏伟蓝图，是事关全民健身和全民健康的发展战略。

With the comprehensive development of economy and society, the improvement of people's living standards, health has become the focus of human society's common concern and has become an important part of the world's pursuit of prosperity and civilization. On March 17, 2016, the Central Committee of the Communist Party of China promulgated the *Thirteenth Five-Year Plan for National Economic and Social Development of the People's Republic of China*, proposing the implementation of healthy China as a national strategy. Many references to the relationships between healthy China and sports in the document. In October 2016, China promulgated the *Healthy China 2030 Plan*, which promoted "Healthy China" to a national strategy for the first time and clarified the ideas and tasks for building "Healthy China" . In the report of the 19th National Congress of the Communist Party of China, it also proposed to "accelerate the construction of a strong country in sports" . This is the first time that the construction of a sports power is clearly put forward in the Party congress. The construction of a sports power is the main goal and grand blueprint for China's sports development in the new era. It is a development strategy that affects the fitness and national health of hundreds of millions of Chinese people.

中国青少年体质健康水平始终是国人关注的焦点，在 2006 年 8 月 19 日举行的“首届中国青少年体质健康论坛”上，国家教育部体育卫生与艺术教育司原司长杨贵仁出示了一组数据：“最近一次全国青少年体质健康调查报告表明，学生肥胖率在过去五年内迅速增加，四分之一的城市男生是‘胖墩’。眼睛近视的比例，初中生接近六成，高中生为七成六，大学生高达八成三。”[1] 中国男性平均身高低于日韩：世界男性平均身高排名中，韩国排第 18 位，平均身高 1.74 米；日本排第 29 位，平均身高 1.707 米；中国男性排第 32 位，平均身高 1.697 米。7 岁到 17 岁的中国男孩平均身高比日本同龄男孩矮 2.54 厘米。从事基础教育工作的全国人大代表吴正宪 2014 年 3 月 6 日列举上述数据并呼吁尽快建立针对校园学生意外伤害的安全保护法规，激发学校让孩子们积极参加体育锻炼的热情，确保学生增强体质。[2]

The health status of Chinese adolescents has always been the focus of Chinese people's attention. At the “First China Youth Physical Health Forum” held on August 19, 2006, Yang Guiren, director of the Department of Sports Health and Art Education of the Ministry of Education, presented a set of data: The latest National Adolescent Physical Health Survey Report showed that the obesity rate of students has increased rapidly in the past five years, and one in four urban boys is “fat”. The proportion of myopia in the eyes is close to 60% for junior high school students and 76% for high school students, 83% for college students. The average height of Chinese males is lower than that of Japan and South Korea: The average height of men in the world ranks 18th in South Korea, with an average height of 1.74 meters; 29th in Japan, with an average height of 1.707 meters; Chinese men rank 32nd, with an average height of 1.697 meters. The average height of Chinese boys between the ages of 7 and 17 is 2.54 cm shorter than that of Japanese boys of the same age. Wu Zhengxian, a NPC deputy who is engaged in basic education, listed the above data on 6th March, 2014 and called for the establishment of safety protection laws for accidental injuries to students on campus as soon as possible, inspiring the school to let children actively participate in physical exercise and ensure that students enhance their physical fitness.

有关资料显示：2014 年全国学生体质健康调研中，全国学生体质健康状况与

[1] 中国青少年体质最近 20 年持续下降 “硬、软、笨”。中国网：http://www.china.com.cn。

[2] 中国男性平均身高矮于日韩 代表疾呼增强学生体质。新华网：http://www.xinhuanet.com。

2010 年相比，部分指标有所好转，中小学生身体素质持续下滑趋势在 2010 年得到初步遏制后，继续呈现“稳中向好”趋势。

According to relevant data, the results of the 2014 National Student Physical Health Survey showed that, compared to 2010, some indicators of students' physical health have improved. The continuous decline in physical fitness of primary and secondary school students was initially curbed in 2010 and continued to show a stable and positive trend.

2018 年 3 月初，北京体育大学教授、运动与体质健康教育部重点实验室主任张一民针对 2017 年全国学生体质健康状况变化特征的抽查结果显示：受教育部体育卫生与艺术教育司委托，从 2015 年到 2017 年，对全国学生体质健康标准测试上报的数据进行抽查复核，并对当年各地各校上报的体测数据进行统计分析和结果比对，抽查对象为从小学一年级到大学四年级的学生。在对比了 2015 年和 2016 年的数据后得出结论，经过多年的努力，我国青少年的体质终于稳步回升了。[1]

At the beginning of March 2018, Zhang Yimin, professor of the Beijing Sport University and director of the Key Laboratory of the Ministry of Sports and Physical Health, said that the results of the survey on the changes in the physical health status of the national students in 2017 indicated that they were entrusted by the Department of Sports Health and Art Education of the Ministry of Education from 2015. By 2017, the data reported by the National Student Physical Health Standards Test will be checked and reviewed, and the physical analysis data and the results of the physical examinations reported by the schools in each year will be compared. The students will be selected from the first grade of primary school to the senior. After comparing the data of 2015 and 2016, it is concluded that after years of hard work, the physical fitness of our young people has finally steadily rebounded.

另 2022 年官方数据显示：我国中小学生体质优良率提升至 55.1%，但肥胖率从 0.2% 升至 7.9%，问题严峻。青少年体质在各项目上表现各异，爆发力和速度、心肺耐力、柔韧性的测试结果显示学生体能发展不均。尽管部分项目成绩优异，整体均衡发展仍需强化。

According to official data from 2022, the physical fitness rate of primary and secondary school students in China has increased to 55.1%, but the obesity rate has risen from 0.2% to 7.9%, indicating a serious problem. The physical fitness of teenagers varies

[1] 艰难的反转。中华人民共和国教育部官方网站：http://www.moe.gov.cn。

in various projects, and the test results of explosive power and speed, cardiovascular endurance, and flexibility show that students' physical development is uneven. Although some projects have achieved excellent results, overall balanced development still needs to be strengthened.

提高大学生体育文化素养是当前高等体育教育亟待解决的重要问题之一。由体质水平、体育意识、体育知识、体育行为、体育品德、体育个性等组成的体育文化素养，是大学生素质教育的重要内容。加强大学生素质教育，提升体质健康水平，训练大学生核心力量，符合时代要求。在大学生学校体育这一最高层次和最后环节推行大学生核心力量训练，理应得到高校的重视与认同。

Improving the quality of college students' sports culture is one of the important issues to be solved urgently in higher physical education. Sports culture literacy consisting of physical fitness level, sports consciousness, sports knowledge, sports behavior, sports morality and sports personality, it is an important content of college students' quality education. Improveing the quality education of college students, improve the health of physical fitness, and train the core strength of college students, in line with the requirements of the times. In the highest level and final link of college students' school sports, the core strength training of college students should be emphasized and recognized by colleges and universities.

核心力量训练能有效改善身体的平衡能力、协调力和柔韧性，对于提升身体素质、改善身体姿势有着很好的作用。核心力量存在于所有运动项目中，所有的体育动作都是以中心肌群为核心的运动链完成的，强有力的核心肌群对运动中的身体姿势、运动技能和专项技术动作起着稳定和支持作用。强大的核心力量可以使运动员在比赛中更好地控制身体，控制运动加速与减速，保持身体的稳定性，还可以提升学生对肌肉的感知和控制能力。

Core strength training can effectively improve the body's balance, coordination and flexibility, and it has a good effect on improving physical fitness and body posture. The core strength exists in all sports project, and all sports activities are completed with a sports chain centered on the middle heart muscle group. Strong core muscle groups stabilize and support body movements, motor skills and special technical movements during exercise. The powerful core strength allows the athlete to better control the body during the game, control the acceleration and deceleration of the movement, maintain the stability of the body, and enhance the students' ability to sense and control the muscles.

近年来，“核心力量训练”在国内外康复训练领域和体能训练领域成果丰硕，在竞技体育领域中被广泛关注。中国备战2008年和2012年奥运会的过程中，“核心力量训练”相关理论作为奥运会备战科技成果被广泛推广到多支国家队应用，但是“核心力量训练”大多数是针对专业运动员或体育专业学生进行的，在普通高校普通学生体育教学中推广极少，普通大学生几乎没有机会接受正规的核心力量训练。

In recent years, “core strength training” has achieved fruitful results in the fields of rehabilitation training and physical training at home and abroad, and has been widely concerned in the field of competitive sports. In the process of preparing for the 2008 and 2012 Olympic Games in China, the theory of “core strength training” has been widely promoted as a scientific and technological achievement for the Olympic Games to many national teams, but most of the “core strength training” is aimed at professional athletes or sports majors. There is very little promotion in ordinary college students’ physical education, and ordinary college students have almost no chance to receive formal core strength training.

核心是“腰椎—骨盆—髋关节”形成的一个整体，具体指膈肌以下、盆底肌以上的中间区域，包括附着在它周围的神经、肌肉、肌腱、韧带和骨骼系统，并受呼吸系统的影响和作用，分布有41对+1块肌肉群。核心柱具体是指肩关节以下、髋关节以上，包括骨盆、胸廓、髋关节和整个脊柱在内的广大区域，形成扩大的“核心区”，分布有55对+1块肌肉群。核心力量是指核心肌群在稳定人体重心、产生和传递力量的基础上，以发展神经支配与控制、整体协调及本体感受性等能力为主要目的而表现出来的力量能力。核心力量训练主要有核心稳定性训练和核心专门性训练2个重要方面，其中核心专门性训练是核心力量训练的本质和重点；核心力量训练方法主要有稳态和非稳态下的徒手训练、自由力量训练以及核心专门性训练等，归结为体位模式训练和动作模式训练。

The core is a whole formed by the “lumbar spine–pelvis–hip joint” , specifically the middle region above the pelvic floor muscle below the diaphragm, including the nerves, muscles, tendons, ligaments and skeletal system attached to it, and is affected by the respiratory system, and there are 41 pairs plus 1 block muscle groups. The “core column” refers specifically to the area below shoulder joint and above the hip joint, including the pelvis, thoracic, hip joint and the entire spine. It is composed of an enlarged “core area” with 55 pairs plus 1 block muscle groups. Core strength refers to the strength of the core muscle group based on the ability to stabilize the body’s weight, generate and transmit strength, and to develop the functions of innervation and control, overall coordination and proprioception. Core strength training mainly includes two important aspects: core stability training and core specialized training. The core specialized training is the essence and focus of core strength training. The core strength training methods mainly include bare-handed training, free strength training and core specialized training in steady state and non-steady state. It comes down to posture mode training and action mode training.

核心力量训练不仅对体育专业运动员有帮助，对普通大学生也有同样的作用，鉴于普通大学生没有像专业运动员那样接受过系统的体能训练，因此探索针对普通大学生的核心力量训练理论与方法就显得尤其重要。核心力量训练和传统力量训练均属于力量训练，将核心力量训练引入高校的体育教学中，不仅有利于大学生掌握各种体育运动技术、改善大学生的身体素质，还能提高大学生参与体育活动的兴趣，丰富其课余文化生活。传统力量训练和核心力量训练既有联系，又存在不同。从根本上讲，传统力量训练侧重于对身体局部力量的提升，而核心力量训练重视对身体整体的协调性和稳定性的控制，在高校体育教育中，体育教师可以采用两种训练方式并用的教学方式。

Core strength training is not only helpful for sports professional athletes, but also for ordinary college students. In view of the fact that ordinary college students do not have professional athletes to receive systematic physical training, it is especially important to explore the core strength training theories and methods for ordinary college students. Core strength training and traditional strength training are both strength training. Introducing core strength training into physical education in colleges and universities is not only conducive to college students mastering various sports techniques, improving the physical quality of college students, but also enhancing the interest of college students in participating in sports activities and enriching the cultural life after school. Traditional strength training and core strength training are both connected and different. Fundamentally, traditional strength training focuses on the improvement of the body's local strength. The core strength training emphasizes the control of the overall coordination and stability of the body. In college physical education, physical education teachers can use two training methods in teaching .

“核心力量训练＋评价量表”的体育课模式有别于专业训练，遵守简单、方便的原则，注重对学生耐力和灵敏度的培养，以提升学生身体的整体素质为最终目的，以教会学生锻炼身体、培养其运动兴趣为目标。能够丰富体育课教学体系，正确评价大学生肌肉状况与核心力量训练效果，激发大学生主动参与体育训练，有效改善当前大学生久坐、运动量不足造成的身体素质低下的状况，提高大学生运动能力，为其终身体育打下坚实的基础，进而增强我国国民体质健康。可以说，核心力量训练是增强学生体质最好的选择。

The physical education mode of the “core area strength training + evaluation scale” is different from professional training. It adheres to the principle of simplicity and convenience, and pays attention to the cultivation of students’ endurance and sensitivity, and improve the overall quality of students’ body as the ultimate goal, to teach students how to exercise and cultivate interest in sports. It can enrich the teaching system of physical education; correctly evaluate the muscle condition and core strength training effect of college students; stimulate college students to actively participate in sports training; effectively improve the current low level of physical quality caused by college students’ sedentary and insufficient exercise; improve the athletic ability of college students; lay a solid foundation for lifelong sports; and thus enhance the health of our national physique. It can be said that core strength training is the best choice to enhance students’ physical fitness.

本书从提高大学生体育文化素养角度，结合高校大学生核心力量训练的现状，从不同训练方法的新视角，系统阐述核心力量的科学化训练依据，论述核心力量训练的概念，制定出实施核心力量训练的运动处方，归纳大学生体质健康测试的评价量表，旨在进一步讨论核心力量训练对高校大学生身体素质的影响，探究有效提升高校体育教学质量及高校大学生体育素质的有效途径。

From the perspective of improving college students’ sports culture literacy, this book combined with the status of college students’ core strength training, from a new perspective of different training methods, systematically expounds the scientific training basis of core strength, discusses the concept of core strength training, and formulates the core strength of implementation. The exercise prescription for training is summarized in the evaluation scale of the college students’ physical health test. It aims to further discuss the influence of core strength training on the physical quality of college students, and explore effective ways to effectively improve the quality of college PE and improve the physical quality of college students.

1 CHAPTER

第一章

核心力量理论

Core Strength Theory

第一节　核心力量

Section 1　Core Strength

对于“核心区域”的概念，国内与国外专家学者的观点大体相近，仅是叙述上存在一些差别。通过查阅资料和走访相关专家，总结出在“核心区域”的界定上主要有以下几种观点。

As for the concept of “core areas” , the views of domestic and foreign experts and scholars are generally similar.There are only some differences in their narration. It is concluded that there are the following views on the definition of core region by consulting materials and visiting relevant experts.

1. 身体核心 Body Core

身体核心（Body Core）通常指日常所说的躯干中间环节，即肩关节以下、髋关节以上，包括骨盆及其周围的小肌肉群，是由腰椎、骨盆、髋关节形成的一个整体，包含29块肌肉。

核心是“腰椎—骨盆—髋关节”形成的一个整体，具体指膈肌以下、盆底肌以上的中间区域，包括附着在它周围的神经、肌肉、肌腱、韧带和骨骼系统，并受呼吸系统的影响和作用，分布有41对+1块肌肉群。

核心柱具体指肩关节以下、髋关节以上，包括骨盆、胸廓、髋关节和整个脊柱在内的区域，又称为扩大的“核心区”，分布有55对+1块肌肉群。

由此看出，核心是指人体的中间环节，具体是肩关节以下、髋关节以上，包括骨盆在内的区域，包括背部、腹部和构成骨盆部的所有肌群。

Core usually refers to what we call the middle part of the torso. It is a small group of muscles below the shoulder and above the hip including the pelvis and its surrounding area. It is a whole body formed by the lumbar, pelvis and hip joint and contains 29 muscles.

The core is an integral part of the lumbar – pelvis – hip joint. It specifically refers to the middle area above the pelvic floor muscle below the phrenic muscle, including nerves, muscles, tendons, ligaments and skeletal systems attached to it, and affected by the respiratory system. There are 41 pairs of +1 muscle groups.

The core column refers to the large area above the hip joint below the shoulder joint, including the pelvis, chest profile, hip joint and entire spine. It's also known as the enlarged "core area", with 55 pairs of +1 muscle groups.

Thus, the core is the middle part of the body. This is the area below the shoulder and above the hip including the pelvis, which contains the muscles of the back, abdomen and all the muscles that make up the pelvis.

2. 核心力量 Core Strength

核心力量存在于所有运动项目中，所有的体育动作都是以核心肌群为基础的，强有力的核心肌群对运动中的身体姿势、运动技能和专项技术动作起到稳定和支持作用。

核心力量是指核心肌群在稳定人体重心、产生和传递力量的基础上，以发展神经支配与控制、整体协调及本体感受性等能力为主要目的而表现出来的力量能力。

Core strength exists in all sports. All the sports movements are based on the core muscle group.Strong core muscle groups can keep your body posture, motor skills and specialized technical movements stable and also support you to finish the movement.

Core strength refers to that on the basis of stabilizing the body's center of gravity, generating and transmitting power, the core muscle groups are mainly aimed at developing the ability of innervation and control, overall coordination and proprioception.

3. 核心骨与核心肌群 Core Bones and Core Muscle Groups

根据国内外学者对运动训练领域核心的界定，人体核心骨主要是脊柱、胸廓骨、髋骨及股骨。脊柱包括颈椎、胸椎、腰椎、骶骨和尾骨；胸廓骨包括胸骨、胸椎和肋骨。两块髋骨、一块骶骨、一块尾骨及连接它们的关节、韧带和软骨共同构成了骨盆。核心骨处于人体的中轴部分，在身体运动过程中起着稳固支撑的作用，决定了附着在核心骨上的肌群的运动。

According to the definition of core areas in sports training academic sector from domestic and foreign scholars, the bones in the core of the human body are mainly the spine, thoracic bone, hip bone and femur.The spine includes the cervical, thoracic, lumbar, sacrum and coccyx. The thoracic bone includes the sternum, thoracic vertebrae, and the rib. The pelvis is made up of two hips, a piece of sacrum, a piece of coccyx, and the joints, ligaments, and cartilage that connect them. The core bone, located in the central axis of the human body, plays a role of solid support during the body movement, which determines the movement of the muscle groups attached to the core bone.

核心肌群包括腹横肌、竖脊肌、腹直肌、腹斜肌、背肌、下背肌、骨盆底肌和交错骨盆，并且髋关节周围的肌肉——臀肌、旋髋肌、股后肌群也属于核心肌群。核心肌群是最接近身体重心的中间环节（腰—骨盆—髋关节），担负着稳定重心、传导力量等职能，是整体发力的主要环节，对上下肢的活动、用力起着承上启下的枢纽作用。强有力的核心肌群，对运动中的身体姿势、运动技能和专项技术动作起着稳定和支持作用。

The core muscle group comprises the transverse abdominis, erector spinae, rectus abdominis, obliques, back muscles, lower back muscles, pelvic floor muscles, and the muscles involved in the cross-pelvic structure. Moreover, the muscles surrounding the hip joint are also recognized as core muscles, including the gluteal muscles, deep rotators of the hip, and the hamstring group. The core musculature represents the central stabilizing complex closest to the body's center of mass, which is called as the lumbo-pelvic-hip complex. It plays a crucial role in maintaining postural stability, transmitting force, and facilitating coordinated movement. This system serves as the primary linkage for force generation and transmission, acting as a crucial intermediary that connects and integrates upper and lower limb dynamics. Notably, a well-developed core musculature is essential for maintaining optimal body posture during movement, refining motor skills, and enhancing the biomechanical execution of specialized athletic techniques by providing structural stability and neuromuscular support.

第二节　核心力量训练概述

Section 2　Overview of Core Strength Training

近年来，核心力量训练在国内外康复训练领域和体能训练领域成果丰硕，广受关注。我国在备战2008年和2012年奥运会的过程中，将核心力量训练相关理论作为奥运会备战科技成果，向多支国家队推广，但是多面向体育专业运动员或体育专业学生开展。

In recent years, core strength training has achieved fruitful results in the sector of rehabilitation training and physical training at home and abroad, and has attracted wide attention.In the process of China's preparation for the 2008 and 2012 Olympic Games, the theory of core strength training as a scientific and technological achievement of Olympic preparations has been promoted to many national teams, but the core strength training is mostly carried out for sports professional athletes or PE majors.

1. 核心力量训练的概念 The Concept of Core Strength Training

核心力量训练和传统力量训练的本质区别在于，传统力量训练侧重于对身体局部力量的提升，而核心力量训练重视对身体整体的协调性和稳定性的控制。

The essential difference between core strength training and traditional strength training is traditional strength training focuses on the improvement of local strength of the body.Core strength training emphasizes control over the overall coordination and stability of the body.

核心力量训练指针对腰椎—骨盆—髋关节周边的核心肌群及深层的小肌肉群进行的力量、稳定、平衡等能力的训练，表现为下背部与腹部肌肉群的协调做功。核心力量训练强调身体的整体性，旨在调动全身整体体能，以核心区域肌群传输能量，稳定运动员动作发挥的水平。

Core strength training refers to the training of strength, stability and balance of the core muscle groups and the deep small muscle groups around the lumbar, pelvis and hip joint. This is shown by the coordination of the lower back with the abdominal muscle groups. Core strength training emphasizes the integrity of the body, aims at mobilizing the whole body energy and transferring energy by the core muscle groups to stabilize the performance level of athletes.

核心力量训练是速度、灵敏、协调等素质训练的基础，而稳定性是核心力量训练的重要内容。因此，核心力量训练的一个重要原则就是在运动中遵循肌群协调做功，要求制订核心力量训练计划时必须强调调动小肌群参与运动的稳定性训练。

the core strength training is the basis of speed, sensitivity, coordination and other quality training. Stability is an important part of core strength training. Therefore, an important principle of core strength training is to follow the coordination of muscle groups, it is required to make a training plan which is necessary to emphasize the stability training of athletes' small muscle groups.

2. 核心力量训练主要部位 Main Parts of Core Strength Training

腰椎—骨盆—髋关节，包括 29 块肌肉，都位于人体的核心部位。这些肌肉在人体运动中起到稳定、传导力量、发力减力等作用，而这些肌群对于人体在移动过程中保持平衡有着重要意义。

The lumbar, pelvis and hip joint, including 29 muscles, are all located in the core areas of the body. These muscles play a role in the human body movement, such as stability, transmission of strength, force reduction and so on, and these muscle groups are important for maintaining balance as the body moves.

竖脊肌位于腰椎—骨盆—髋关节之中，对脊柱和骨盆的稳定性具有重要意义。同时，竖脊肌还与腹肌互相配合，为人体在静止和运动中完成各种技术动作提供支持和保证，在此过程中，骨盆肌群也参与工作。

The erector spine lie in the middle of the lumbar, pelvis, and hip joint. It is important for the stability of the spine and pelvis. At the same time, the erector spine muscle and the abdominal muscle also cooperate to provide support and guarantee for the completion of various technical movements of the human body in stillness and motion, during the process, the pelvic muscle group also participates in the work.

骨盆带是由骨组成的一个环状的架构，附着其上的肌肉对于稳定骨盆的正常位置非常重要，特别是对于下肢加速、减速和髋关节内收外展的运动项目来说。

Pelvic girdle is composed of a ring of bone architecture.The attached muscles are important to stabilize the normal position of the pelvis, especially for acceleration and deceleration of lower limb and hip joint adduction and abduction.

这些骨相接融合，形成耻骨联合。由于骨盆和骶髂关节的柔韧性较差，在运动时，肌肉收缩和拉长对其施加的压力增加，加上内收肌力的薄弱，极易对耻骨造成损伤。因此，只有稳定住骨盆才能保证髋关节肌群有效工作。

These bones are join and fuse together to form the symphysis pubis.Since the pelvis and sacroiliac joints are less flexible,the increased pressure exerted by muscle contraction and elongation during exercise, together with the weakness of adductor muscle force. It can easily cause damage to the pubis.Therefore, it is necessary to stabilize the pelvis to ensure the effective functioning of the hip muscle groups.

3. 核心力量训练类型与作用 Type and Function of Core Strength Training

核心力量训练主要包括核心稳定性训练和核心专门性训练两个重要方面。其中核心专门性训练是核心力量训练的本质和重点。

Core strength training mainly includes core stability training and core specialization training. Among them, core specialization training is the essence and emphasis of core strength training.

核心力量训练能有效改善身体的平衡能力、协调能力及曲线，对于提升身体素质、改善身体姿势有着很好的作用。强大的核心力量可以使学生在比赛中更好地控制身体，控制运动加速与减速，保持身体的稳定，还可以提升其平衡能力和肌肉的感知能力。

Core strength training can effectively improve the body's balance, coordination and curve. It is good for improving the physical quality and body posture. A strong core allows students to better control their bodies during a race, control movement acceleration and deceleration, and keep their bodies stable. It also improves balance and muscle perception.

第三节 大学生核心力量训练解析

Section 3 Analysis of College Students' Core Strength Training

我国高校把培养能适应社会需求和工作需要的高素质、复合型人才作为教育重点。然而，在实际工作中，大学生的体育文化素养，特别是身体素质有待进一步提高。目前，我国大学生因久坐、运动量不足，身体素质整体状况并不理想，出现肺活量不足、肥胖、近视等问题。

Universities in China take the training of high quality and interdisciplinary talents who can meet the social needs and work needs as the key point of education. However, the improvement of college students' physical culture accomplishment, especially physical quality, needs to be further strengthened. Chinese college students are currently suffering from problems such as lack of lung capacity, obesity and myopia due to long sitting time and insufficient exercise.

1. 大学生核心力量训练的现状 Current Situation Core Strength Training for College Students

有数据显示，我国青少年体质连续 25 年下降。2013 年，第六次全国学生体质与健康调研数据显示，中国大学生身体素质继续呈缓慢下降趋势，体质测试数据显示，学生的肺活量、爆发力、下肢力量等都低于《国家学生体质健康标准》及格水平。2014 年 6 月 11 日，教育部出台的《高等学校体育工作基本标准》(教体艺〔2014〕4 号) 规定：高校要将学生体育学业成绩和体质测试结果作为招生录取的重要依据；强调学生测试成绩低于 50 分不能毕业；测试成绩评定达到良好及以上者，方可参加评优与评奖。教育部公布的《关于 2010 年全国学生体质与健康调研结果公告》(教体艺〔2011〕4 号) 中同样提到，大学生身体素质呈现继续缓慢下降趋势。大学生核心力量素养在普通高校体育教学中常被忽视，学生几乎没有机会接受正规的核心力量训练。

Statistics show that the physical fitness of Chinese teenagers has declined for 25 consecutive years. In 2013, the sixth national survey data on students' physical fitness and health showed that the physical quality of Chinese university students continued to decline slowly. According to the physical fitness test data, students' lung capacity, explosive power, lower limb strength, etc. are all lower than the *National Standards for Physical Health of Students*. The Ministry of Education set the *Basic Standards for Physical Education in Colleges and Universities* on June 11, 2014. It says colleges and universities should take students' physical education achievements and physical fitness test results as the important basis for enrollment. It stressed that students with test scores below 50 cannot graduate. Only those who have achieved good and superior performance in the evaluation of test can participate in the evaluation of excellence and awards.Also mentioned in the Ministry of Education's *Announcement on the Results of A National Survey on Students' Physical Fitness and Health in 2010*, the physical fitness of college students continues to decline slowly.College students' core strength quality is often neglected in physical education teaching in colleges and universities, students hardly have access to normal core strength training.

由此可见，如何提高大学生身体素质，形成一套促进大学生积极训练的体系，已经成为高校与体育教育工作者面临的一个极其严峻的课题。

Thus it can be seen, how to strengthen the physical quality of college students and form a training system to encourage students to participate in training actively has become an extremely serious issue facing the staff of university and sports education.

2. 大学生核心力量训练的意义 The benefit of Core Strength Training for College Students

核心力量训练在运动员训练中运用广泛，一般来讲，大学生的体能训练强度与时间不及运动员。因此，对大学生进行核心力量训练教学，对提高大学生的身体素质及综合素质作用显著。

Core strength training is widely used in athlete training.Generally speaking, the intensity and time of physical training of college students is not as much as that of athletes.Therefore, the teaching of core strength training in college students plays a significant role in improving their physical and comprehensive qualities.

在我国，体育教师可以采用核心力量训练和传统理论训练两种训练方式并用的教学方式。将核心力量训练引入高校的体育教学中，不仅能丰富学生的课余锻炼内容，还能改善学生的身体素质。

In China, physical education teachers can adopt a teaching approach that combins both core strength training and traditional strength training method. Adding the core strength training into the physical education in colleges and universities, it can not only enrich students’ extracurricular exercise content, but also improve students’ physical quality.

全面而系统的核心力量还可以有效降低学生运动时的受伤率。核心力量训练对于提升学生的协调性和平衡性有重要作用，并且教学效果显著。核心力量测试与评估是评价核心稳定性、诊断核心专门性力量、发现弱链环节、修正训练计划、改进训练方法以及合理规划总体训练目标的有效途径。

Comprehensive and systematic core strength can also effectively reduce the injury rate when students participate in sports. Core strength training plays an important role in improving the coordination and balance of students, and the teaching effect is remarkable. Core strength testing and evaluation is an effective way to evaluate core stability, diagnose core specialized strength, discover weak links, revise training plan, improve training method and plan the overall training target reasonably.

3. 大学生核心力量训练对身体素质的影响 The Influence of College Students' Core Strength Training on Their Physical Quality

（1）对力量素质的影响。

(1) The Effect on Strength Quality.

力量素质是大学生进行体育活动的最基本素质之一。大学生要完成简单或复杂的运动，必须依靠身体的力量。核心力量的训练主要就是为了锻炼学生身体上部肌肉群的力量，从而使上体肌群和背部肌肉的力量得到全面提高。在核心力量训练的过程中，可以使用多种训练方法和运动器材，为小肌肉群设计专门的训练方法，从而从整体上提升学生的力量。

Strength quality is one of the basic quality for college students to take part in sports activities.To accomplish simple or complex sports, college students must rely on physical strength.Core strength training is mainly to train the strength of the upper body muscle groups, so that the upper body muscle groups and back muscle strength can be improved comprehensively.In the process of core strength training, multiple training methods and sports equipment can be used to design special training methods for small muscle groups, so as to increase students' strength.

（2）对速度素质的影响。

(2) The Effect on Speed Quality.

核心力量训练注重对学生神经和肌肉协调性的训练，通过加强学生的神经感受能力来提高学生的快速反应能力。学生在进行体育锻炼时，需要保持身体重心的稳定性，进而实现速度的提高。另外，核心部位位于身体的上部与下部的结合处，对力量在身体上下部位的传导、发力、减力起承上启下的作用。

Core strength training emphasize nerve and muscle coordination training to strengthen the students' neurosensory capacity, so as to improve the students' quick reaction ability.When doing physical exercises, students need to maintain the stability of the body to achieve speed improvement.In addition, the core is located in the joint of upper and lower parts of the body, which plays a connecting role in the conduction generation and reduction of force in the upper and lower parts of the body.

（3）对灵敏素质的影响。

(3) The Effect on Agility Quality.

灵敏性是在运动中遇到外界环境突然发生变化时，人体能够快速做出空间位置和运动方向的改变，同时还能在不减少运动力量的情况下，保持身体平衡、重心稳定。核心力量训练关注的是学生在运动中急停、快速变方向的瞬间，对身体重心稳定性的训练，既能提高核心肌群的力量，又能提高神经系统的控制能力和协调性。灵敏性是学生在运动过程中神经感应、运动技能和其他素质的综合反应。通过核心力量训练，能提高学生感受器官的反应能力，以增强学生的灵敏能力。在大学生体质测试中，学生能对测试中出现的异常状况及时做出反应，避免出现不必要的伤害事故。

Agility is the ability of the human body to quickly change its spatial position and movement direction to maintain balance and stable gravity without reducing exercise strength in the face of sudden changes in the external environment during exercise. The core strength training focuses on the training of the body gravity stability in the moment when the students are in a hurry stop and quick direction changing. It can not only improve the strength of the core muscle groups, but also improve the control and coordination of the nervous system. Agility is a synthetical reaction of students' nerve induction, motor skills and other qualities during exercise.Through the core strength training, students can improve the response of the sensory organs to enhance their agility. In the physical test of college students, students can respond to abnormal conditions in time to avoid unnecessary injury accidents.

（4）对柔韧素质的影响。

(4) The Effect on Flexibility Quality.

人们普遍认为，儿童时期是身体柔韧性最好的阶段，随着年龄的增长，柔韧性会不断降低。其实，大学生的柔韧性经过专门的训练是可以提高的。现实中，大学生缺乏户外锻炼，对体育运动缺乏兴趣，进而导致一进行体育运动就会出现运动过量、运动疲劳，肌肉、韧带拉伤等情况。因此，通过核心力量训练提高学生的柔韧性十分重要。在大学生体质测试中，有一些可以检查学生身体柔韧性的项目。因此，在核心力量训练过程中，适当进行一些提高柔韧度的训练项目，可以提高学生的柔韧性，以此来降低运动损伤现象发生的可能性。

It is generally accepted that childhood is the best period of physical flexibility.

As you get older, your flexibility decreases. In fact, the flexibility of college students can be improved by professional training. In reality, college students lack of outdoor sports, they are not interested in sports.This will lead to overexertion, fatigue, muscle and ligament strain, and other similar conditions. Therefore, it is important to improve students' flexibility through core strength training.In the college students physical fitness test, there are some events to check students' physical flexibility. In the process of core strength training, some flexibility training can improve students' flexibility, so as to reduce the possibility of sports injury.

(5)对耐力素质的影响。

(5) The Effect on Endurance Quality.

大学生体质健康测试中设有跑步项目，尤其是长跑，主要是为了发展学生的耐力素质，一些学生经常在长跑中因为体力不支、耐力不够未能完成测试或者测试不达标。在核心力量训练过程中，通过上下肢的协调性训练，对学生进行有氧训练，提高人体肌群的携氧能力，使人体在长时间的运动中能通过呼吸来调节自己的运动状态，降低疲劳程度。因此，核心力量训练不仅能增强学生的一般耐力，还能提高学生的速度耐力。

College students' physical fitness test is set with some running items, especially long-distance running, it is mainly to develop students' endurance quality. In the long-distance running test, some students fail to complete the tests or fail to meet the standards because of lack physical strength and lack endurance. In the process of core strength training, through the coordinated training of students' upper and lower limbs, the students were given aerobic training, to improve the oxygen-carrying capacity of the human muscle groups. So that people can adjust their sports status through breathing during long-term exercise and reduce the degree of fatigue.Therefore, core strength training can not only enhance students' general endurance ability, but also improve their speed endurance ability.

CHAPTER 2

第二章

核心力量训练热身活动、放松活动

The Warm – up Exercise and Relaxation Training of Core Strength Training

第一节　热身活动、放松活动的理论意义

Section 1　Theoretical Significance of Warm – up Exercise and Relaxation Training

1. 热身活动解析 The Analysis of Warm – up Exercise

热身活动是指在运动之前，采用短时间、低强度的动作，对身体的肌肉进行预热，提升身体的温度，加快血液循环，让身体的各个部位做好充分的准备，从而使身体更快地适应接下来即将进行的剧烈运动，降低自身受伤的概率。热身活动看似简单，但是对于运动来说却极其重要。

Warm-up exercise is trying to warm the muscles, raise the body temperature and get the blood pumping by doing some low intensity exercise in short time and low-intensity before the training，and reduces the risk of injury. Although warm-up exercise seems simple,it is extremely important.

热身活动可以分为两种，第一种是静态热身活动，是指将肌肉缓慢牵拉至一定长度，并在一定时间内（20～30 秒）保持这种牵拉感的拉伸方法；第二种是动态热身活动，是指在完成一系列动作的过程中，有控制地将肌肉牵拉较短时间（1～2 秒）并重复多次的拉伸方法。热身的意义体现在以下几个方面。

Warm-up exercise can be divided into two parts. The first part is of static warm-up. That refers to stretching muscles slowly to a certain length and maintaining the tension for a certain time（usually 20-30 seconds）. The second part is dynamic warm-up.That refers to stretching muscles with control for a short time（1-2 seconds）and repeated several times during doing a series of movements. The significance of warm-up exercise is refected in the following aspects.

（1）动员心脏活动，加强呼吸机能。

（2）改善肌肉的血流供应，激活肌纤维。

（3）降低肌肉黏滞性、增强弹性，防止受伤。

（4）提高体内物质代谢效率。

（5）提高中枢神经和肌肉的兴奋性。

（6）加快主动肌与拮抗肌的收缩与放松。

（7）改善肌肉力量与爆发力。

（8）提高肌肉反应速度。

(1) Mobilize and strengthen cardiac activity and respiratory function.

(2) Improve muscle blood flow supply and activate muscle fibers.

(3) Reduce muscle viscosity, enhance elasticity, and prevent injuries.

(4) Strengthen the body material metabolism process.

(5) Increase the excitability of central nervous system and muscles.

(6) Accelerate the contraction and relaxation of agonist and antagonistic muscles.

(7) Improve muscle strength and explosive power.

(8) Increases muscle response rate.

2. 放松活动解析 The Analysis of Relaxation Training

运动过后的“冷却”方法——放松活动，如同运动之前的“预热”一样不可忽视，有利于达到运动的功效。现实生活中，我们常常看到有的人做完剧烈运动之后，不做放松活动就离开了，这样的运动是不完整、不科学的。运动后马上静止不动，会使高度运转的神经、肌肉得不到缓冲，这时候的激素水平、血压等都处于较高状态，对心脑血管很不好。运动后做放松活动，会让机体各个部位逐渐适应从运动到停止运动这一变化过程，保护身体健康。

The “Cooling” after exercise, we call it relaxation training.It is as important as the warm-up exercise, can not be ignored. It is conducive to achieving the effect of exercise. Some people finish their exercise without relaxation training.That is incomplete and unscientific. If we take a rest after exercise immediately,our nerve and muscles will be unbuffered.Meanwhile the hormone level, blood pressure are still keep a high rate.It will be harmful to heart and cerebral vessels.Do some relaxation training after exercise will help bodies gradually adapt to the great changes in the external environment , and protect our bodies.

放松活动是指在体育锻炼后所采用的一系列放松练习和运动后按摩等恢复手段，目的是消除疲劳、恢复体能、提高锻炼效果。放松活动的意义主要体现在以下几个方面。

Relaxation training refers to adopt a series of relaxation exercises and post-exercise massage and some other recovery methods after doing physical exercises. The purpose is to eliminate fatigue, recovery and improve exercise effects.The significance of relaxation is reffected in the following aspects.

（1）放松活动可以促使机体迅速偿还"氧债"。运动时机体需要大量的氧气供代谢使用，同时机体在代谢过程中会产生大量废气（如二氧化碳）随呼吸排出体外。若运动较为剧烈，机体往往出现氧气短时间内供应不足的情况，这就使机体欠下"氧债"，体内二氧化碳也不能及时排出体外而堆积。如果在剧烈运动结束后做一些放松活动，使呼吸保持一定强度，就可以及时吸入氧气、呼出二氧化碳，保持机体酸碱平衡，有利于迅速消除疲劳。

(1) Relaxation can prompt the body to get back from the anaerobic zone quickly. During exercise, a lot of oxygen is required for metabolic use. And during the metabolic process, the body will produce a lot of waste gas（such as carbon dioxide）. The waste gas will be exhaled with breathing. Due to the vigorous exercise, the body often has a short of oxygen. That causes the body to get into the anaerobic zone. Meanwhile, the carbon dioxide in the body cannot be released out of the body in time and it accumulates in body. If the exercisers do some relaxation training to keep breathing after doing exercise, the exercisers' breathing will keep strong so that the exercisers can inhale oxygen and exhale carbon dioxide in time. That will help to maintain the body acid- base balance and eliminate fatigue quickly.

（2）放松活动可以使紧张的肌肉得到放松。在运动中，肌肉毛细血管大量开放，肌肉高度紧张。如果激烈运动后立即静止不动，肌肉内淤积的血液就不能及时流回心脏，造成肌肉僵硬、疲劳不易消除。相反，运动后做一些放松活动，使运动慢慢缓和下来，或通过按摩挤压肌肉和穴位，能够使肌肉得到充分的放松和休息。

(2) Relaxation training can relax the tense muscles. During exercise, a large numbers of muscle capillaries open up and muscles become highly tense. If we take a rest after exercise immediately, the accumulated blood in the muscles will not flow back to the heart in time which can also lead to muscle stiffness and fatigue can not be easily eliminated.If the exercisers can do some relaxation training after exercise to make the

body cool down or squeeze to muscles and acupoints massage, to make the muscle fully relaxed and rested.

（3）放松活动可以促进血液循环，使躯体和内脏尽快地恢复到安静状态。运动后立即停止肌肉活动，四肢就无法利用肌肉的收缩将血液送回心脏，这时心脏仍跳动很快并继续将血液送至四肢，这种不平衡会造成这样的结果：一方面，四肢特别是腿部血流不畅；另一方面，脑部和其他脏器因回心血量减少而无法获得心脏送去的血液。这时，轻者出现头晕、乏力，重者出现晕厥。因此，剧烈运动后，放松活动是保证躯体和内脏运动平衡的重要措施。

(3) Relaxation training can promotes positive blood flow and make the body and viscera return to resting state as soon as possible. Stopping muscle activity immediately after exercise, the blood in the extremities cannot use muscle contraction to send it back to the heart. Meanwhile, the heart is still beating fast and continue to send the blood back to the extremities. This imbalance can result: on the one hand, extremities, especially the legs, are clogged with blood. On the other hand,insufficient blood supply to the brain and other organs because of the reduced venous return. That will cause dizziness, fatigue, even fainting. Therefore, it is very important to do relaxation training after strenuous exercise.

（4）放松活动可以缓解紧张的情绪。人体在运动之后，需要逐步恢复到相对安静的状态，缓解锻炼时的紧张心理。从心理学角度看，运动之后的放松活动可以逐渐消除紧张的心理。良好的心境对人的行为具有促进作用，而消极的心境则可能使原先感觉很有兴趣的事情变得索然无味。

(4) Relaxation training can relieve tension. After exercise, the body needs to regain relative composure smoothly and relieve mental tension during exercise.From a psychological point of view, doing relaxation training after exercise can help restore mental tension. Good mood can promote people's behavior,opposite, a negative state of mind can make things that previously seemed interesting become boring.

第二节　训练前热身活动

Section 2　Pre-training Warm-up

一般而言，不同运动项目的热身活动，在具体内容和时间上会有所不同，但所有热身活动大体上都是使全身各主要肌肉群、关节、韧带得到充分活动，目的在于逐步提高大脑皮层的兴奋性，使体温和肌肉温度上升，以防止在剧烈运动时可能造成的运动损伤。

In general, the warm-up varies from different sports.But all the warm-up training is trying to activate major muscle groups, joints and ligaments throughout the body. The purpose of warm-up training is to increase the excitability of the cerebral cortex, so that the temperature of body and muscle will rise and it will reduce the probability of injury during the exercise.

锻炼者在热身时可以进行一些全身性运动，如慢跑、身体各大关节的活动、肌肉韧带的动力性拉伸练习等，要着重活动一下运动中可能使用的关节。准备活动的时间和强度根据身体的健康水平和运动时的反应来确定，一般通过 5～10 分钟练习，感觉身体发热，微微出汗，有点气喘就可以了。

The exercisers can do some full-body exercises as warm-up, such as jogging, move the joint, stretch the muscle ligament and so on.The exercisers should pay more attention to the joint which may be used in the flowing movement. The time of warm-up training depends on how healthy your body is and how your own body react during the exercise. Usually,after 5-10 minutes of warm-up, the body temperature will rise. Meanwhile the exercisers sweat slightly and feel a little breathless.That will be fine.

1. 关于热身活动的一些问题 Some Questions About Warm-up

（1）拉伸：拉伸分为静力性拉伸和动力性拉伸两种。一般在训练前热身活动时，最好以动力性拉伸练习为主，因为静力性拉伸过多会影响速度和爆发力的表现。对于运动后的恢复，最好针对主要运动肌群进行一些静力性拉伸练习，这样能消除疲劳，提高恢复效果，也能增强身体柔韧性。

(1) Stretching: Stretching can be divided into static stretching and dynamic stretching.Generally, it is better to do dynamic stretching before exercise. Because static stretching will affect exercises’ speed and explosive force. For recovery after exercise, it is better to do some static stretching exercises for the main muscles.It can help to eliminate fatigue, improve the recovery effect and increase flexibility.

（2）热身活动和正式运动之间休息的时间不要太长：休息时间过长，已经活动热的身体就会转凉，这时就需要重新做热身活动。

(2) Don’t rest for a long time after warm-up: If exercisers rest too long, the body will cool down.After that the warm-up will not be helpful. Exercisers need to do warm-up exercises again.

（3）热身活动时间不是一成不变的：热身活动一般占总运动时间的 10%～20%，

即运动 1 小时，热身活动需要做 6～12 分钟。但这个时间不是固定的，如跑步锻炼的热身活动环节可自行安排。另外，天气对热身活动也是有影响的，夏季天气炎热，身体容易进入兴奋状态，可以减少热身活动时间；冬季天气寒冷，热身活动时间要适当延长。一定要保证将身体机能充分调动起来，肌肉和关节都被激活。这种情况下才能更好地预防运动损伤。

(3) The time of warm-up is not fixed: Generally, the time of warm-up accounts for 10% to 20% of the total exercise time.For example, if you want to exercise for 1 hour, 6-12 minutes warm-up is required. But this is not fixed, the warm-up of running exercise can be arranged by oneself.In addition, the weather also has an influence on the warm-up. In summer, when the weather is hot, the body can easily enter the excited state, which can reduce the warm-up time. In winter,the weather is cold, the time of warm-up should be extended.The exercisers must ensure the body in full swing and the muscles and joints are activated.In that case, we can reduce the risk of injury.

2. 热身活动动作示例 Examples of Warm-up Actions

热身活动的动作较多，在此仅列举几个常见的全身性快速热身活动动作：波比跳、开合跳、高抬腿、平板支撑、快速仰卧撑（图 2-2-1 至图 2-2-5）。

There are so many warm-up moves. In this column, only a few common full-body quick warm-up actions are listed: burpee、jumping jacks、high knee lift、plate support and fast push-ups (Fig.2-2-1 to Fig.2-2-5).

图 2–2–1　波比跳
Fig.2–2–1　Burpee

图 2-2-2 开合跳
Fig.2-2-2 Jumping jacks

图 2-2-3 高抬腿
Fig.2-2-3 High knee lift

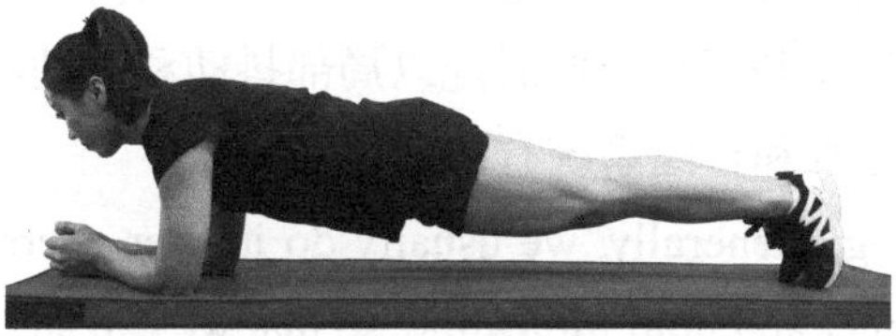

图 2-2-4 平板支撑
Fig.2-2-4 Plate support

图 2-2-5 快速俯卧撑
Fig.2-2-5 Fast push-ups

以上动作可单独作为热身活动，也可组合起来，每个动作 1 分钟或选择适合自己的时间作为热身活动项目。当然，热身活动前需先活动各个关节，特别是常用的腕关节、踝关节、膝关节等。

You can take the previous moves separately as a warm-up, or you also can string them together by yourself. Doing them each for 1 minute or more if you like, and combine them as a warm-up.But before doing warm-up, exercisers should move the joints, especially the joints may used, for example, the wrist, ankle, knee and so on.

第三节　训练后放松活动

Section 3　Past-training Relaxation

1. 常见放松活动方式 Common Ways of Relaxation

（1）静态拉伸：一般在运动后进行，慢慢地将身体的某个部位移动至另一个部位，并保持一定时间，从而牵拉某块肌肉。

（2）滚泡沫轴：泡沫轴是一个廉价的按摩器，但效果很好。

（3）动态拉伸：动态拉伸常用于运动前的热身。

（4）整理活动：一般包括摆臂、转腰、抖腿等，目的是促进血液回流，放松肌肉。

（5）推拿按摩及温水浴：一般应在锻炼后 20～30 分钟后进行。开始可先做轻推摩、擦摩、揉捏、按压和叩打，同时配以局部抖动和被动活动。在 30～40℃的温水中浸泡洗浴，对心脏和神经系统有镇静作用。

(1) Static stretching: Generally, we usually do it after exercise. Slowly move one part of the body to another and hold for awhile, so that we can stretch muscles.

(2) Using foam rollers: The foam rollers is a cheap masseur, and has good effect.

(3) Dynamic stretching: Dynamic stretching is often used for warm-up before exercise.

(4) Coding-down exercises: Generally include swing arms, twisting the waist and shaking legs.The purpose is to promote blood flow and relax your muscles.

(5) Massage and warm bath: Generally,we usually do it 20 to 30 minutes after exercise.At first, we usually do some massage, rubbing, kneading, pressing and tapping,at the same time,it is better to do some chattering and passive motion. Bathing in warm water about 30-40℃ will have a calming effect on cardiomotility and the nervous system.

2. 放松活动动作示例 Examples of Relaxation Training

了解拉伸对于运动的重要意义后，可以尝试一次完整的拉伸。拉伸在运动中活动较多的肌肉，直到感觉它完全绷紧，保持 15～30 秒即可。放松的动作方法较多，在此仅列举几个常见的全身性快速放松动作（图 2-3-1 至图 2-3-4）。

Once you understand the importance of stretching for exercises, you can try to stretch. You can stretin muscle used more in activities until you feel it fully tense and hold for 15 to 30 seconds.There are many relaxation movements. In this column, only a few common full-body quick relaxation movements are listed（Fig.2-3-1 to Fig.2-3-4）.

（1）**坐姿转体背部拉伸：**拉伸时吐气放松，拉伸至极致停留 15 秒。

(1) Sitting with your back muscles stretched: Exhaling and relaxing, stretching to the maximum and holding for 15 seconds.

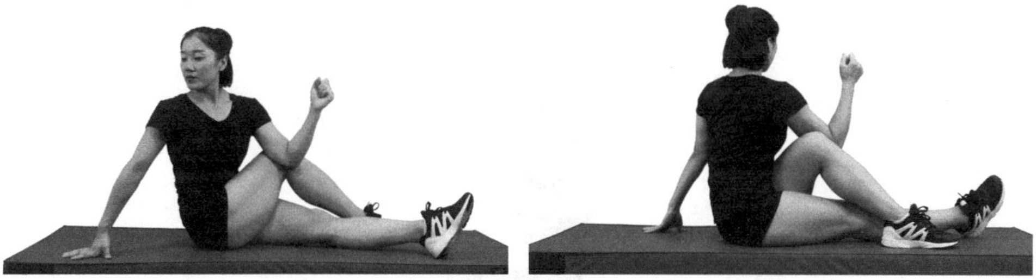

图 2–3–1　坐姿转体背部拉伸

Fig.2–3–1　Sitting with your back muscles stretched

（2）**腹直肌拉伸：**均匀呼吸，延展腹直肌。

(2) Stretching the rectus abdominis: breathing evenly, and stretching the rectus abdominis.

图 2–3–2　腹直肌拉伸

Fig.2–3–2　Stretching the rectus abdominis

（3）**臀部拉伸：**在延伸极限的地方停留 15 秒，匀速呼吸。

(3) Stretching gluteus: Stretching to the maximum and holding for 15 seconds with your breathing constant.

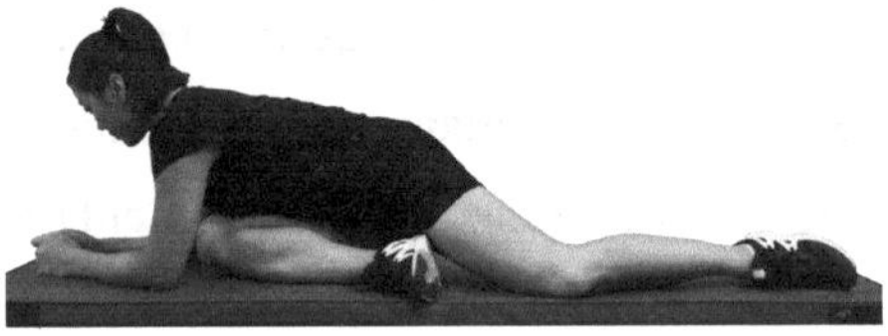

图 2-3-3　臀部拉伸
Fig.2-3-3　Stretching gluteus

（4）**大腿前侧拉伸**：支撑腿保持稳定站立，身体站直，尽量不弯曲。

(4) Stretching front thigh muscles: Standing steadily and upright, trying not to bend.

图 2-3-4　大腿前侧拉伸
Fig.2-3-4　Stretching front thigh muscles

CHAPTER 3

第三章

核心力量徒手训练

Bare – handed Core Strength Training

第一节　腹部与核心肌群组合训练

Section 1　Combination Training Abdomen and Core Muscle Group

1. 单腿两头起　One Leg V-ups

锻炼部位：腹部。

Muscles exercised: Abdominal muscles.

动作要领：

（1）双手伸直，腹肌发力起身。

（2）起身时腿部伸直，下背部贴地，手触摸到小腿，另一侧腿不能离开地面。

（3）起身时呼气，还原时吸气。（图 3-1-1）

Behavioral essentials:

(1) Keep your arms straight and use the power from your abdominal muscle to do V-ups.

(2) When you up,you should keep your leg straight and your lower back touching the ground, the hand touches the lower leg and the other leg cannot leave the ground.

(3) Exhale when you up and inhale when you return. (Fig.3-3-1)

负荷强度：2 组，每组 20 次，每组间歇 10 秒。

Intensity: 2 sets in all, each set for 20 times, then taking a 10-second break.

注意事项：

（1）抬腿至 90°，手脚触碰。

（2）腰部贴地。

（3）另一条腿放松。

Attentions:

(1) Lift your leg to 90° and make your hands touch the foot.

(2) Keep your waist touching the ground.

(3) Keep the other leg relax.

图 3-1-1 单腿两头起

Fig.3-1-1 One leg V-ups

2. 倒蹬车 Retrograde Pedalling

锻炼部位：腹部。

Muscles exercised: Abdominal muscles.

动作要领：

（1）动作尽量缓慢，不可用力蹬腿。

（2）下背部贴近地面。

（3）保持均匀呼吸。（图 3-1-2）

Behavioral essentials:

(1) Move as slowly as possible. and don't push your legs hard.

(2) Keep your lower back touching the ground.

(3) Keep breathing evenly. (Fig.3-1-2)

负荷强度：2 组，每组 30 次，每组间歇 8 秒。

Intensity: 2 sets in all, each set for 30 times, then taking a 8-second break .

注意事项：

（1）腰部挤压手背。

（2）臀部稍稍抬起。

（3）勾起脚尖。

（4）动作不宜过快。

Attentions:

(1) Squeeze the back of your hand at the waist.

(2) Hip lift slightly.

(3) Hook your tiptoes.

(4) Move slowly.

图 3–1–2　倒蹬车
Fig.3–1–2　Retrograde pedalling

3. 仰卧单车 Floor Biking

锻炼部位：腹部。

Muscles exercised: Abdominal muscles.

动作要领：

（1）下背部始终贴近地面。

（2）转动上身将手肘朝前送，交替触碰对侧膝盖。

（3）用力提膝，将膝盖靠近手肘。转身时呼气，中间位置时吸气。（图 3-1-3）

Behavioral essentials:

(1) Keep your lower back touching the ground.

(2) Turn your upper body forward with your elbows, touch the opposite knee alternately.

(3) Lift your knee hard and bring it close to your elbow. Exhale as you turn and inhale in the middle. (Fig.3-1-3)

负荷强度：2 组，每组 20 次，每组间歇 10 秒。

Intensity: 2 sets in all, each set for 20 times, then taking a 10-second break.

注意事项：

（1）双肩离地。

（2）腰部贴地。

（3）手肘触碰膝盖。

（4）左右转动上身。

Attentions:

(1) Get your shoulders off the ground.

(2) Keep your waist touching the ground.

(3) Make your elbows touch the knees.

(4) Turn the upper body from side to side.

图 3–1–3 仰卧单车

Fig.3–1–3 Floor Biking

4. 简化俄罗斯转体 Simplified Russian Transformation

锻炼部位：腹部。

Muscles exercised: Abdominal muscles.

动作要领：

（1）双肩转动带动手臂转动。

（2）下背部挺直，上背部略微弯曲。

（3）手接触地面两侧，目光随手的转动而移动。

（4）转身时呼气，身体转正时吸气。（图 3-1-4）

Behavioral essentials:

(1) Turn your shoulders to move your arms.

(2) Keep the lower back straight and the upper back slightly bent.

(3) Make the hand touch both sides of the ground, keep the eyes move with your

hands.

(4) Exhale as you turn around, inhale as you turn back. (Fig.3-1-4)

负荷强度：2 组，每组 20 次，每组间歇 10 秒。

Intensity: 2 sets in all, each set for 20 times, then taking a 10-second break.

图 3-1-4　简化俄罗斯转体
Fig.3-1-4　Simplified Russian transformation

注意事项：

（1）保持双手触地。

（2）保持双脚着地。

Attentions:

(1) Keep yours hands touching the ground.

(2) Keep yours feet touching the ground.

5. 俯卧交替抬腿 Lift Your Legs Alternately in the Prone Position

锻炼部位：腹部。

Muscles exercised: Abdominal muscless.

动作要领：

（1）肩部稍稍抬离地面，双手垫于腰下做支撑。

（2）下背部贴近地面，双腿伸直，勾起脚尖。

（3）均匀呼吸。（图 3-1-5）

Behavioral essentials:

(1) Lift the shoulders slightly off the ground and place your hands under your waist for support.

(2) Keep the lower back close to the ground, with legs straight and toes hooked.

(3) Breath evenly. (Fig.3-1-5)

负荷强度：2 组，每组 15 次，每组间歇 10 秒。

Intensity: 2 sets in all, each set for 15 times, then taking a 10-second break.

注意事项：

（1）拇指垫于腰下。

（2）双腿伸直，勾起脚尖。

（3）肩部稍微抬离地面。

Attentions:

(1) Put your thumb under your waist.

(2) Keep legs straight and toes hooked.

(3) Lift the shoulders slightly off the ground.

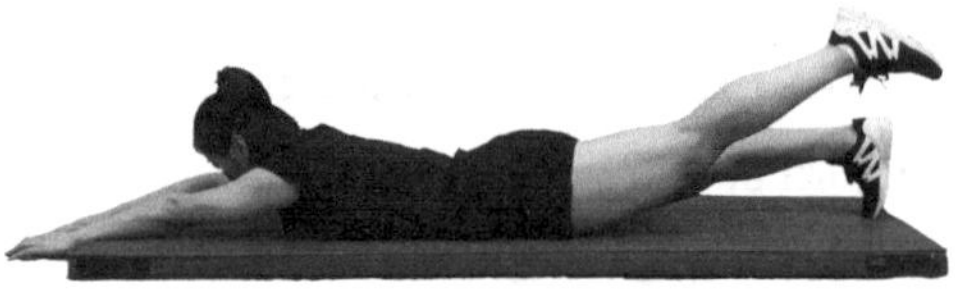

图 3-1-5 俯卧交替抬腿

Fig.3-1-5 Lift your Legs Alternately in the prone position

6. 俯卧提膝 Knee Lifting in the Prone Position

锻炼部位：腹部。

Muscles exercised: Abdominal muscles.

动作要领：

（1）腿向前提起时腹部发力。

（2）拱起下背部。

（3）提腿时呼气，还原时吸气。（图 3-1-6）

Behavioral essentials:

(1) Use the abdominal power when leg lifts forward.

(2) Arch the lower back.

(3) Exhale as you lift your leg and inhale as you return. (Fig.3-1-6)

负荷强度：2 组，每组 20 次，每组间歇 10 秒。

Intensity: 2 sets in all, each set for 20 times, then taking a 10-second break.

注意事项：

（1）收腹使下背部拱起。

（2）紧绷肩膀。

Attentions:

(1) Abdomen in to arch the lower back.

(2) Tighten the shoulder.

图 3-1-6 俯卧提膝

Fig.3-1-6 Knee Lifting in the Prone Position

7. V 字支撑转体 V-Swivel

锻炼部位：腹部。

Muscles exercised: Abdominal muscles.

动作要领：

（1）腰腹始终保持挺直，收紧腰腹。

（2）转动时双肩随身体转动伸出，转动骨盆将腿收回。

（3）摸脚时呼气，回正时吸气。（图 3-1-7）

Behavioral essentials:

(1) Keep waist and abdomen straight and tighten waist and abdomen.

(2) The shoulders extend out as the body rotates, and the legs pull back by rotating the pelvis.

(3) Exhale when you touch your foot and inhale when you return. (Fig.3-1-7)

负荷强度：2 组，每组 15 次，每组间歇 10 秒。

Intensity: 2 sets in all, each set for 15 times, then taking a 10-second break.

注意事项：

（1）双肩左右旋转。

（2）收紧腹部。

（3）臀部上侧支撑身体。

Attentions:

(1) Rotate your shoulders left and right.

(2) Tighten the abdomen.

(3) Use upper hip to support the body.

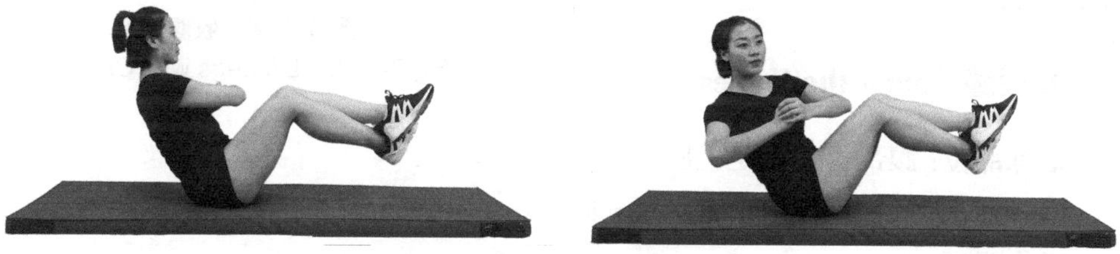

图 3-1-7　V 字支撑转体

Fig.3-1-7　V-swivel

8. 收腹举腿 Lift Legs with Crunches

锻炼部位：腹部。

Muscles exercised: Abdominal muscles.

动作要领：

（1）仰卧，身体伸直处于水平位置上，两臂伸直。

（2）双手自然置于体侧，然后收腹向上举起双腿至垂直部位。

（3）慢慢放下成原来姿势。（图 3-1-8）

Behavioral essentials:

(1) Lie on your back. Keep your body straight and your arms straight.

(2) Place your hands naturally on the sides of the body and lift your legs up to the vertical position.

(3) Slowly lay down to the start position. (Fig.3-1-8)

负荷强度：3～4 组，每组 20～30 次，每组间歇 30 秒。

Intensity: 3-4 sets in all, each set for 20-30 times, then taking a 30-second break.

注意事项：

（1）双腿绷紧固定，动作不宜太快。

（2）借助惯性摆动双腿。收腹举腿动作速度要快，放腿速度应慢。

（3）多次重复该动作能有效发展髋关节屈肌群和腹肌力量。

Attentions:

(1) Tighten and fix the legs, do not move too fast.

(2) Use inertia to swing your legs. Lift your legs quickly, put them down slowly.

(3) Doing this repeatly can effectively develop the strength of the hip flexor and abdominal muscle.

图 3–1–8　收腹举腿

Fig.3–1–8　Lift Legs with Crunches

9. 摸膝 Touch the Knees

锻炼部位：腹部，尤其是上腹部。

Muscles exercised: Abdominal muscles, especially upper parts.

动作要领：

（1）腰部贴地，臀部略微抬起。卷腹时重力压在腰上。

（2）双手始终伸直，使用双手触膝。

（3）摸膝时吸气，下落时呼气。（图 3-1-9）

Behavioral essentials:

(1) Make the waist touching the ground, raise the hips slightly. The weight on the waist when making crunches.

(2) Keep your arms straight and touch your knees with your hands.

(3) Exhale as you touch your knees and exhale as you lay down. (Fig.3-1-9)

负荷强度： 2 组，每组 25 次，每组间歇 10 秒。

Intensity: 2 sets in all, each set for 25 times, then taking a 10-second break.

注意事项：

（1）手臂尽可能伸直。

（2）保持腰部贴地。

（3）以肩膀将手臂向前推。

Attentions:

(1) Keep your arms as straight as possible.

(2) Keep the waist touching the ground.

(3) Push your arms forward with your shoulders.

图 3-1-9　摸膝

Fig.3-1-9　Touch the Knees

10. 西西里卷腹 Sicilian Crunches

锻炼部位： 腹部，尤其是上腹部。

Muscles exercised: Abdominal muscles, especially upper parts.

动作要领：

（1）缓慢抬起上半身，不可用手臂力量。

（2）卷腹时手竖直向上举高。

（3）下背部要始终贴紧地面。

（4）卷腹时呼气，落下时吸气。（图 3-1-10）

Behavioral essentials:

(1) Slowly lift yoor upper body without using arm strength.

(2) Raise your hands vertically when you make crunches.

(3) Keep your lower back touching the ground.

(4) Exhale as you make crunches and inhale as you lay down. (Fig.3-1-10)

负荷强度： 2 组，每组 20 次，每组间歇 10 秒。

Intensity: 2 sets in all, each set for 20 times, then taking a 10-second break.

注意事项：

（1）双手垂直上举。

（2）腰部贴地。

（3）臀部微微抬起。

Attentions:

(1) Raise your arms vertically.

(2) Keep the waist touching the ground.

(3) Lift hip slightly.

图 3-1-10　西西里卷腹
Fig.3-1-10　Sicilian Crunches

11. 平板支撑 Plank

锻炼部位：腹部。

Muscles exercised: Abdominal muscles.

动作要领：

（1）保持头、肩、背、臀、膝、脚踝成一条直线。

（2）手肘朝脚的方向用力，脚尖用力向前勾起，与地面摩擦力对抗。

（3）前臂用力按地面。

（4）均匀呼吸。（图 3-1-11）

Behavioral essentials:

(1) Keep the head, shoulders, back, hips, knees and ankles in a straight line.

(2) The elbow apply force in the direction of your feet and your tiptoes are against the ground friction.

(3) The forearm pressed hard against the ground.

(4) Breath evenly. (Fig.3-1-11)

负荷强度：2 组，每组 40 秒，每组间歇 10 秒。

Intensity: 2 sets in all, each set for 40 seconds, then taking a 10-second break.

注意事项：

（1）用力撑高身体。

（2）收紧腹部。

Attentions:

(1) Push your body up.

(2) Tighten your abdomen.

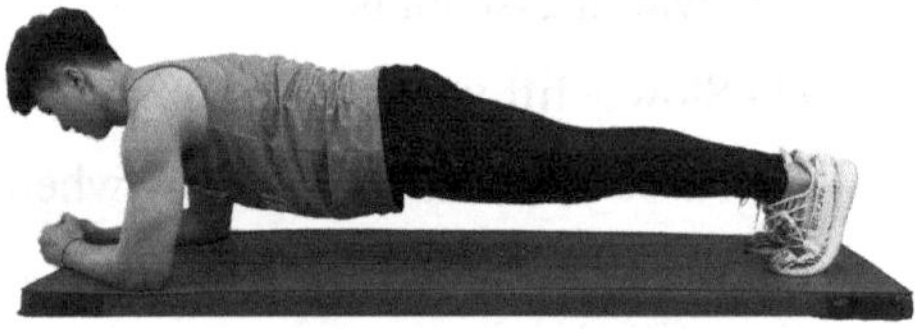

图 3-1-11　平板支撑
Fig.3-1-11　Plank

12. 屈腿收腹 Perform a Crunch with Legs Bent

锻炼部位：腹部，尤其是下腹。

Muscles exercised: Abdominal muscles, especially lower parts.

动作要领：

（1）双手撑于臀部两侧。

（2）双腿运动时，臀部跟着前后卷动。

（3）收腿时吸气，伸腿时呼气。（图 3-1-12）

Behavioral essentials:

(1) Put hands on both sides of the hip.

(2) When your legs move, your hips roll back and forth together.

(3) Inhale as you bend your legs, exhale as you stretch them. (Fig.3-1-12)

负荷强度：2 组，每组 20 次，每组间歇 10 秒。

Intensity: 2 sets in all, each set for 20 times, then taking a 10-second break.

注意事项：

（1）颈部保持竖直。

（2）腹部收紧。

（3）大腿尽可能靠近胸部。

（4）用臀部上侧支撑身体。

Attentions:

(1) Keep your neck straight.

(2) Tighten your abdomen.

(3) Keep your thighs as close to your chest as possible.

(4) Use your upper hips to support your body.

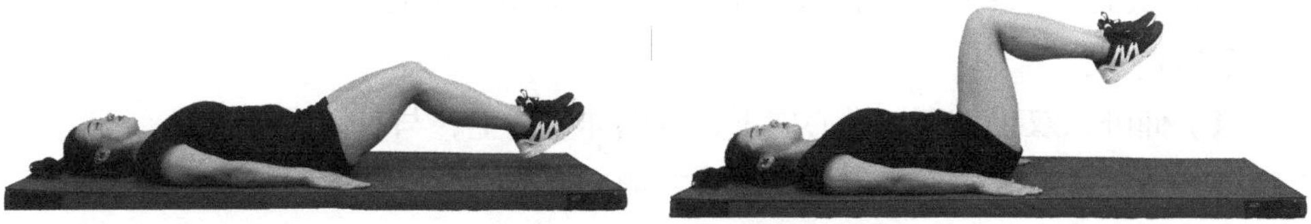

图 3–1–12 屈腿收腹

Fig.3–1–12 Perform a Crunch with legs bent

13. 反向卷腹 Reverse Crunch

锻炼部位：腹部，尤其是下腹。

Muscles exercised: Abdominal muscles, especially lower parts.

动作要领：

（1）双手抱头仰卧，卷起臀部时，以下背部用力挤压地面。

（2）腿下放时，控制好身体，控制好力量，不要利用惯性。

（3）卷腹时吸气，双腿下落时呼气。（图 3-1-13）

Behavioral essentials:

(1) Lie on your back with both hands holding your head, roll up your hips, and press your lower back firmly against the ground.

(2) When lowering your legs, control your body, control your strength, and do not use inertia.

(3) Inhale as you roll up, exhale as you down. (Fig.3-1-13)

负荷强度：2 组，每组 30 次，每组间歇 12 秒。

Intensity: 2 sets in all, each set for 30 times, then taking a 12-second break.

注意事项：

（1）双腿紧绷固定。

（2）双手抱头。

（3）抬起臀部。

Attentions:

(1) Keep your legs tight and steady.

(2) Hug your head with both hands.

(3) Lift your hip.

图 3–1–13　反向卷腹

Fig.3–1–13　Reverse crunch

14. 十字交叉 Cross

锻炼部位：腹肌，肋间肌。

Muscles exercised: Abdominal muscle, intercostal muscle.

动作要领：

（1）仰卧，双手打开，掌心向下，双腿伸直向上，与身体成 90°。

（2）头稍微离开地面，然后把腿往右侧地面放，与身体成“L”形。

（3）在腿触到地面前，抬起，回到起始位置。

（4）然后向另一侧做相同动作。如果觉得难度太大，可以屈膝完成相同动作。（图 3-1-14）

Behavioral essentials:

(1) Lie on your back, hands open, palms down, keep legs straight up at 90 degrees with your body.

(2) Leave your head slightly off the ground and put your legs on the right side of the ground, in an L-shape with your body

(3) Lift up the legs before touching the ground, then return to the initial position.

(4) Then do the same thing on the other side. If you find it too difficult,you can bend your knees. (Fig.3-1-14)

负荷强度：2～3 组，每组 30～40 次，每组间歇 40 秒。

Intensity: 2-3 sets in all, each set for 30～40 times, then taking a 40-second break.

注意事项：

（1）注意身体平衡。脚尖伸直，双手平举。双腿不要弯曲。

（2）身体与双腿之间尽量保持垂直。

Attentions:

(1) Keep balance. And, keep your toes straight, hands straight. Don't bend your legs.

(2) Try to stay upright between your body and your legs.

图 3-1-14　十字交叉

Fig.3-1-14　Cross

15. 侧卧提臀 Side Lying Hip Lift

锻炼部位：腹斜肌，肋间肌。

Muscles exercised: The oblique abdominal muscles, the intercostal muscles.

动作要领：

（1）右侧卧，右肘撑地，左手平举，躯干与腿在同一平面。

（2）左腿叠加在右腿上，提高臀部。

（3）保持身体平直，然后缓慢落下，单侧做 10 次，然后换另外一侧。（图 3-1-15）

Behavioral essentials:

(1) Lie on your right side with your right elbow on the floor, lift your left hand flat. Keep your torso and legs flat.

(2) Make the left leg superimpose on the right leg, raise the hips.

(3) Keep your body flat, then down slowly. Finish 10 times on one side, and then switch to the other. (Fig.3-1-15)

负荷强度：2～3 组，每组 20 次，每组间歇 30 秒。

Intensity: 2-3 sets in all, each set for 20 times, then taking a 30-second break.

注意事项：

（1）上身收紧时尽量不要前倾。

（2）尽量不要放松臀部肌肉。

Attentions:

(1) Try not to lean forward when the upper body tightening.

(2) Try not to relax hip muscles.

图 3-1-15　侧卧提臀

Fig.3-1-15　Side lying Hip lift

第二节　背部与核心肌群组合训练

Section 2　Combination Training of the Back and Core Muscle Group

1. 山羊挺身 Back Extension

锻炼部位：上背部。

Muscles exercised: Upper back.

动作要领：

（1）开始准备：俯卧，伸展身体，双臂横展，双腿伸直。

（2）动作过程：拉长脊骨，将手臂往身体后方伸展，慢慢抬高肩膀。（图 3-2-1）

Behavioral essentials:

(1) Warm-up: lie flat on the stomach, stretch your body, keep your arms spread and legs straight.

(2) Action process: stretch the spine, and stretch your arms toward the back of your body, then slowly elevate your shoulders. (Fig.3-2-1)

负荷强度：4 组，每组 15～20 次，每组间歇 30～45 秒。

Intensity: 4 sets in all, each set for 15-20 times, then taking 30-45-second break.

注意事项：

（1）始终保持腹部和臀部收紧。

（2）抬高肩膀后，颈部和脊柱应成一条弧线。

（3）俯身时自由下落。

（4）动作不宜过快。

Attentions:

(1) Always keep your abdomen and hips tight.

(2) After elevating the shoulder, you should maintain your neck and spine in an arc.

(3) Keep free falling when you bending your body.

(4) Action should not be too fast.

图 3-2-1　山羊挺身

Fig.3-2-1　Back extension

2. 立式耸肩 Vertical Shrug

锻炼部位：上背部。

Muscles exercised: Upper back.

动作要领：

（1）身体直立，两臂张开，稍宽于肩。肩部尽量后夹，两臂放松。

（2）耸起两肩，主要是收缩斜方肌，静止 1 秒，松下肩，重复此动作。（图 3-2-2）

Behavioral essentials:

(1) Stand upright, keep your arms open and slightly wider than the shoulders. Clip your shoulders tightly as far as possible while making your arms relaxing.

(2) Raise your shoulders mainly to contract the trapezius muscle, keep motionless for 1 second and relax your shoulders, repeat the action. (Fig.3-2-2)

负荷强度： 4 组，每组 12 次，每组间歇 30～45 秒。

Intensity: 4 sets in all, each set for 12 times, then taking a 30-45-second break.

注意事项：

（1）保持手臂放松，上臂用力抬起肩膀。

（2）肩部没有尽可能后夹，不能完全发挥斜方肌的作用。

（3）训练时全神贯注，双手自然下垂，略展开。

（4）耸肩时要完全依靠收缩斜方肌产生的力量，两肘不能弯曲。

Attentions:

(1) Keep your arms relaxing while using the upper arms to lift the shoulders.

(2) The trapezius's function cannot be fully exerted if your shoulders haven't clipped as much as possible.

(3) Be concentrated on the training, keep your hands naturally dropping and slightly outward.

(4) Don't bent your elbow, you must rely on the force energized by the contraction of the trapezius muscles to raise your shoulders.

图 3–2–2　立式耸肩

Fig.3–2–2　Vertical shrug

3. 俯身平地两头起 Bend Over the Body and Lift Your Head and Legs

锻炼部位： 整个背部。

Muscles exercised: Back.

动作要领：

（1）俯卧，腹部着地，保持双臂向前伸展，双腿向后伸直。

（2）抬头，呼气，双臂和双腿同时抬离地面约 10 厘米，坚持 1 秒，然后慢慢放下双臂和双腿，回到原来的位置。（图 3-2-3）

Behavioral essentials:

(1) Lie flat on the stomach, keep your arms stretched forward and legs backward straightly.

(2) Raise your head, exhale, and lift your arms and legs about 10 cm above the ground for 1 second, then slowly lower your hands and hind legs to their original position. (Fig.3-2-3)

负荷强度：4 组，每组 15～20 次，每组间歇 30～45 秒。

Intensity: 4 sets in all, each set for 15-20 times, then taking a 30-45-second break.

注意事项：

（1）如果刚开始做整个动作有困难，可以先试试左手和右手同时抬起，坚持 1 秒。

（2）换右手和左腿同时抬起，坚持 1 秒。

（3）注意做动作时，要低下头，以免颈部受伤。

Attentions:

(1) If you have difficulty performing the entire movement at the beginning, you can try lifting both your left and right hands simultaneously for 1 second.

(2) Lift both your right hand and left leg at the same time and hold on for 1 second.

(3) Pay attention to lowering your head when performing movements to avoid neck injuries.

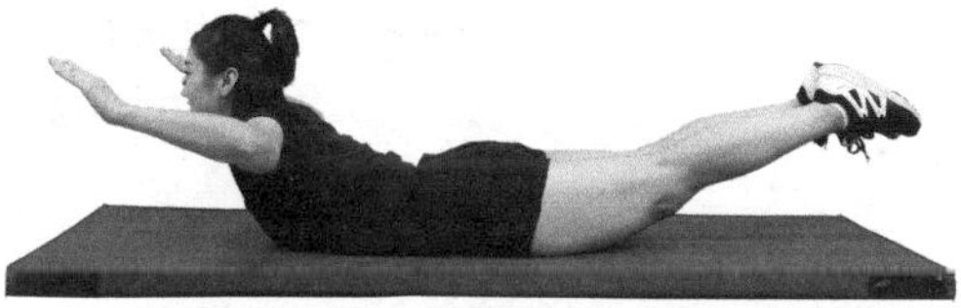

图 3-2-3 俯身平地两头起

Fig.3-2-3 Bend over the body and lift your head and legs

4. 俯卧背腿 Lie Flat on Your Stomach while Raising Your Legs

锻炼部位：腰部、背部。

Muscles exercised: Waist and back.

动作要领：

（1）俯卧在地板或垫子上，两腿并拢伸直。

（2）髋部支撑，两臂伸直置于体侧，连续做两腿向后上振起动作。（图 3-2-4）

Behavioral essentials:

(1) Prostrate on the floor or mat, keep your legs straight and close to each other.

(2) Use your hips as a supporting point, stretch the arms straightly and put them besides your body, keep your legs performing up-an-down actions continuously.

(Fig.3-2-4)

负荷强度：2～3组，每组20～30次，每组间歇40秒。

Intensity: 2-3 sets in all, each set for 20-30 times, then taking a 40-second break.

注意事项：

（1）收腹将骨盆保持在中立位置，腰部放松。

（2）两腿尽量向上振起。

Attentions:

(1) Keep the abdomen-contracting and put your pelvis in a neutral position, relax the waist.

(2) Lift your legs as high as possible.

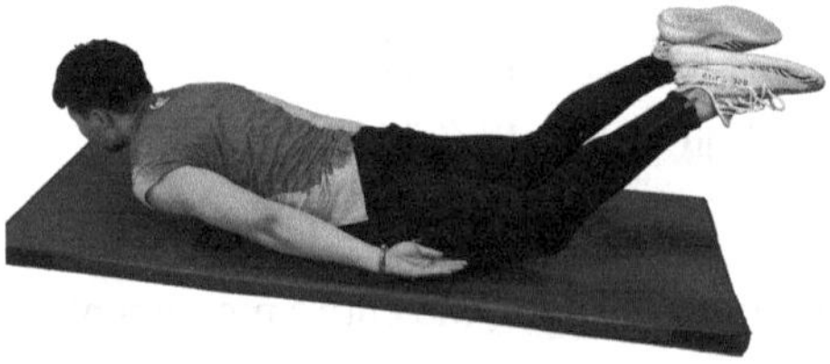

图 3-2-4　俯卧背腿

Fig.3-2-4　Lie flat on your stomach while raising your legs

5. 猫式伸展 Cat Stretch

锻炼部位：背部、腰部。

Muscles exercised: Back and waist.

动作要领：

（1）身体呈跪地姿势，双手撑地。

（2）拱起上背部，低头。

（3）胸部下沉到最低，仰头，全身放松。

（4）含胸、尽力弓背至最高点。（图 3-2-5）

Behavioral essentials:

(1) The body is in a kneeling position, with both hands supporting the ground.

(2) Arch up your back and lower your head.

(3) Lower your chest to the lowest point, look up, and relax your whole body.

(4) Containing chest, try to arch your back to the highest point. (Fig.3-2-5)

负荷强度：2～3组，每组15～20个，每组间歇30～40秒。

Intensity: 2-3 sets in all, each set for 15-20 times, then taking 30-40 seconds break.

注意事项：

（1）脚背伸直，注意调整呼吸。

（2）呼吸调整不好，动作速度不易掌握。

Attentions:

(1) Straighten your instep, pay attention to regulate your breath.

(2) The speed of the movement is not so easy to act if your breath cannot be regulated.

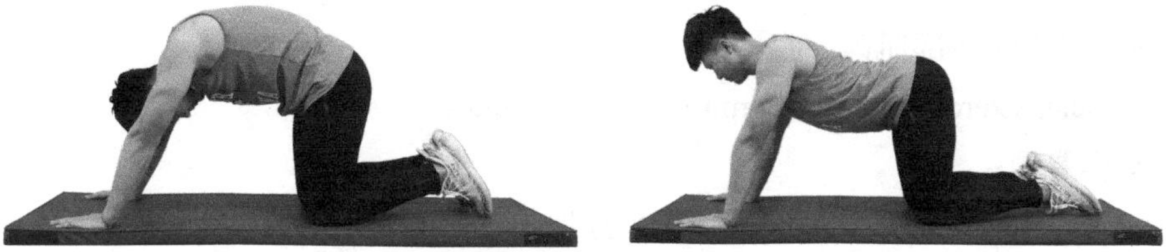

图 3–2–5 猫式伸展

Fig.3–2–5 Cat stretch

第三节 腹部与背部组合训练

Section 3 Combination Training of the Abdomen and Back

1. 连续跳跃 Successive Jump

锻炼部位：腰部、下肢。

Muscles exercised: Waist and lower limbs.

动作要领：

（1）可用单腿或双腿进行水平跳。

（2）上体正直、蹬地有力、动作连贯。（图 3-3-1）

Behavioral essentials:

(1) You can jump with the one-leg or the double-legs.

(2) Keep the upper part of the body upright, push off the ground forcefully and perform these actions coherently. (Fig.3-3-1)

负荷强度：3～4 组，每组 30～40 次，每组间歇 1 分钟。

Intensity: 3-4 sets in all, each set for 30-40 times, then taking a 1-minute break .

注意事项：

（1）膝盖微屈，双腿放松。

（2）跳跃过程中，不宜前后左右晃动。

Attentions:

(1) Keep your knees slightly bent and legs relaxed.

(2) It is not advisable to shake back and forth during the jumping exercise.

图 3–3–1 连续跳跃
Fig.3–3–1 Successive jump

2. 侧卧剪刀腿 Lateral Scissor Kicks

锻炼部位：臀部肌肉、腹斜肌。

Muscles exercised: Gluteus muscles and obliques.

动作要领：

（1）左侧卧，左手支撑头部，右手撑地，尽可能高抬右腿。

（2）身体保持在一个立面上，在最高点保持 3 秒，回落。

（3）做到力竭然后换右侧，动作相同。（图 3-3-2）

Behavioral essentials:

(1) Keep left lateral recumbent position, use your left hand to support your head and right hand prop up to the ground, then elevate your right leg highly as much as possible.

(2) Keep your body erected, hold the posture for 3 seconds at the highest point, then fall back.

(3) Do this continuedly until you feel exhausted and then change the right side, and continue to do the same action. (Fig.3-3-2)

负荷强度：2～3 组，每组 20 次，每组间歇 30 秒。

Intensity: 2-3 sets in all, each set for 20 times, then taking a 30-second break.

注意事项：

（1）脚尖尽量朝下，绷直腿，利用臀部侧面发力，使身体扭曲。

（2）双腿尽量保持水平面内平衡。

Attentions:

(1) You must keep your tiptop downward as far as possible, straight legs, maintain your body contorted powered by one side of your hips.

(2) Keep your legs balanced as far as possible in the horizontal plane.

图 3–3–2　仰卧剪刀腿
Fig.3–3–2　Lateral scissor kicks

3. 站立提膝 Stand Upright and Lift Your Knee

锻炼部位：腹部及腿部肌肉。

Muscles exercised: Muscles in the abdomen and legs.

动作要领：

（1）自然站立，双手平举，与肩同宽，在最高点保持约 3 秒，然后缓慢放下。

（2）换右腿，动作相同，提起时呼气，落下时吸气。（图 3-3-3）

Behavioral essentials:

(1) Stand up with your hands flat, shoulder width apart, hold for about 3 seconds at the highest point, then slowly lower down.

(2) Change the right leg, then do the same action, exhale when lifting, inhale when dropping. (Fig.3-3-3)

负荷强度：2～3 组，每组 20 次，每组间歇 20 秒。

Intensity: 2-3 sets in all, each set for 20 times, then taking 20 seconds for intermittence.

注意事项：

（1）保持身体平衡。

（2）膝盖尽量抬高。

（3）上身挺直，切勿倾斜。

Attentions:

(1) Keep your body balanced.

(2) Raise your knee as high as possible.

(3) Keep the upper part of your body straight and upright, do not lean.

图 3–3–3　站立提膝
Fig.3–3–3　Stand upright and lift your knee

4. 陆地游泳 Land Swimming

锻炼部位：大腿肌群、下背部。

Muscles exercised: Thigh muscles group and lower back.

动作要领：

（1）俯卧，双手朝前自然平伸，尽可能抬高右腿和左臂。

（2）最高点处保持 3 秒，缓慢放下。

（3）相同姿势，抬高左腿和右臂。（图 3-3-4）

Behavioral essentials:

(1) Lie prone, keep your hands straightly forward, raise your right leg and left arm highly as much as possible.

(2) Hold for 3 seconds at the vertex , slowly put your hands and legs down.

(3) Raise your left leg and right arm as same as the right leg and left arm do. (Fig.3-3-4)

负荷强度：2～3 组，每组 15～20 个，每组间歇 45 秒。

Intensity: 2-3 sets in all, each set for 15-20 times, then taking a 45-second break.

注意事项：

（1）双手不要弯曲。

（2）腿和臂不可同侧。整个过程中保持身体贴着地面。

（3）头微微抬起以保持身体平衡。

Attentions:

(1) Keep your hands unbend.

(2) You cannot do this with the same hands and legs, and you should keep your body close to the ground during whole process.

(3) You can slightly raise your head to balance the body.

图 3–3–4　陆地游泳

Fig.3–3–4　Land swimming

5. 仰卧起坐 Sit-ups

锻炼部位：腰部、腹部、髂腰肌。

Muscles exercised: The waist, the abdomen and the iliopsoas.

动作要领：

（1）仰卧在地板或体操垫上，使身体处于水平位置。

（2）腿伸直，双手抱头，然后上抬上体至垂直位置。

（3）慢慢后倒成原来的姿势，重复 5 次。（图 3-3-5）

Behavioral essentials:

(1) Lying in supine posture on the floor or gym mat to keep the body in a horizontal position.

(2) Straighten legs, hold your head in your hands and then lift the upper part of your body to the vertical position.

(3) Lower your upper body slowly to the starting position,and repeat the action 5 times. (Fig.3-3-5)

负荷强度：2～3 组，每组 30～40 次，每组间歇 40 秒。

Intensity: 2-3 sets in all, each set for 30-40 times, then taking a 40-second break.

注意事项：

（1）注意腹部发力，身体、肩部、上下背部依次离地。

（2）避免颈部僵硬，全身应协调发力。

Attentions:

(1) Use strength from abdomen, lift the body, shoulders, upper and lower back off the ground in turn.

(2) Do not let your neck be stiff, and you should coordinate your body.

图 3–3–5　仰卧起坐
Fig.3–3–5　Sit–ups

6. 臂屈伸 Chair Drips

锻炼部位：胸大肌、三角肌、肱三头肌、腹直肌、腹横肌。

Muscles exercised: Pectoralis major, deltoid, triceps muscle of arm, rectus abdominis, musculus trasversus abdominis.

动作要领：

（1）双臂支撑于凳上，上体保持直立。

（2）双脚开立与肩同宽，小腿与大腿、大腿与躯干各呈 90° 。

（3）肘关节慢慢弯曲，同时肩关节伸屈，使身体逐渐下降至最低位置。

（4）稍停片刻，两臂用力撑起至还原。（图 3-3-6）

Behavioral essentials:

(1) Sit down on the edge of the chair and place your hand behind you.The upper body remains upright.

(2) Both feet are shoulder-width apart.The lower leg and thigh, thigh and torso are at 90 degrees.

(3) Slowly bend the elbow joints, while the shoulder joints are extended and flexed, so that the body gradually drops to the lowest position.

(4) Pause for a moment and push your arms up until you are back. (Fig.3-3-6)

负荷强度：2～3 组，每组 15～20 次，每组间歇 20 秒。

Intensity: 2-3 sets in all, each set for 15-20 times, then taking 20 seconds for intermittence.

注意事项：

（1）身体不可随意晃动，要保持平衡。

（2）下放的速度要慢，身体尽量降低。

Attentions:

(1) Do not shake your body and will. Keep balance.

(2) Lower it slowly and make your body as low as possible.

图 3–3–6 臂屈伸

Fig.3–3–6 Chair drips

7. 臀桥 Glute Bridge

锻炼部位：腹部、腰部。

Muscles exercised: Abdomen and waist.

动作要领：

（1）臀部抬起时，上背部支撑地面。

（2）臀部抬起时保持膝、髋、肩呈一条直线。（图 3-3-7）

Behavioral essentials:

(1) Raise your hips, the upper back supports the ground.

(2) The knees, hips, shoulders in a straight line when the hip is raised. (Fig.3-3-7)

负荷强度：2～3 组，每组 20～30 次，每组间歇 30 秒。

Intensity: 2-3 sets in all, each set for 20-30 times, then taking 30 seconds for intermittence.

注意事项：

（1）腰部贴地，脚跟踩地。

（2）手臂下压，腰腹发力，臀部上挺。

Attentions:

(1) Let your waist attach to the ground and heels support the body.

(2) Lower your arms, exert force on your waist and abdomen, and lift your hips.

图 3–3–7 臀桥

Fig.3–3–7 Glute bridge

4 CHAPTER

第四章

核心力量单一器械训练

Core Strength Training with Single Instrument

第一节　平衡垫训练

Section 1　Balanced Cushions Training

1. 平衡下蹲 Balance Squat

锻炼部位：臀大肌、股直肌、腹直肌、阔筋膜张肌。

Muscles exercised: Gluteus maximus, the rectus femoris, the rectus abdominis, and the tensor fascia latae.

动作要领：

（1）平衡垫放于双脚下，上体正直，双手体前平屈。

（2）大小腿呈 150° 弯曲，两腿分开与肩同宽，屈膝半蹲。（图 4-1-1）

Behavioral essentials:

(1) Place the balance pad under both feet, keep the upper body upright, and bend both hands flat forward.

(2) The thigh and calf should be bended at 150 degrees, stand with your feet shoulder-width apart,then bend your knee and keep half squat. (Fig.4-1-1)

负荷强度：4 组，每组 15 秒，每组间歇 15 秒。

Intensity: 4 sets in all, each set for 15 seconds, then taking a 15-second break.

注意事项：

（1）大腿尽量与地面保持水平，如果身体无法保持平衡，下蹲时角度小一些也行。

（2）注意膝盖的位置，不要内扣或者外翻。

Attentions:

(1) Try to keep your thighs level with the ground. If the body can not maintain balance, smaller angle is also acceptable.

(2) Pay attention to the knee position, do not buckle or out turn.

图 4-1-1　平衡下蹲
Fig.4-1-1　Balance squat

2. 综合平衡下蹲 Comprehensive Balance Squat

锻炼部位： 臀大肌、股直肌、腹直肌、阔筋膜张肌。

Muscles exercised: Gluteus maximus, the rectus femoris, the rectus abdominis, and the tensor fascia latae.

动作要领：

（1）两手侧平举，上体正直，屈膝半蹲，大小腿呈 150° 弯曲。

（2）双脚开立，略宽于肩，各踩一个平衡垫。（图 4-1-2）

Behavioral essentials:

(1) Raise both hands horizontally, keep your upper body upright, bend your knees and half-squat, and bend your legs at a 150 degrees angle.

(2) Open your feet slightly wider than your shoulders and step on a balance pad each foot. (Fig.4-1-2)

负荷强度： 训练 4 组，每组 15 秒，每组间歇 15 秒。

Intensity: 4 sets in all, each set for 15 seconds, then taking a 15-second break.

注意事项：

（1）膝盖朝向脚尖。

（2）膝盖不要内扣或外翻。

（3）下蹲至大腿与地面平行或略高于平行的位置。

（4）下蹲时，腰背伸直，核心肌肉收紧。

Attentions:

(1) Point your knees toward your toes.

(2) Do not push your knees inward or outward.

(3) Squat down to a position where your thighs are parallel to or slightly above it.

图 4-1-2　综合平衡下蹲
Fig.4-1-2　Comprehensive balance squat

(4) When squatting, straighten your waist and back, and tighten your core muscles.

3. 平衡箭步蹲 Balanced Lunge

锻炼部位：臀大肌、股直肌、腹直肌、阔筋膜张肌。

Muscles exercised: Gluteus maximus, the rectus femoris, the rectus abdominis, and the tensor fascia latae.

动作要领：

（1）两腿前后分开，两手叉腰，屈膝后撤半蹲。

（2）上体正直，大小腿呈 150° 弯曲，平衡垫放于前脚脚下。（图 4-1-3）

Behavioral essentials:

(1) Let one of your legs in front of the other, then bend the knees and keep half-squat with arms akimbo.

(2) Place the balance pad under your forefeet, and keep the upper body straight, then bend your legs at 150 degrees. (Fig.4-1-3)

负荷强度：4 组，每组 15 秒，每组间歇 15 秒。

Intensity: 4 sets in all, each set for 15 seconds, then taking a 15-second break.

图 4-1-3　平衡箭步蹲
Fig.4-1-3　Balanced lunge

注意事项：

（1）脚后跟发力。

（2）竖直蹲起。

（3）脚尖点地支撑。

Attentions:

(1) Use the power from the heels.

(2) Squat vertically.

(3) Stand on your toes.

4. 飞鸟支撑 Supporting the Body Like a Flying Bird

锻炼部位：臀大肌、股直肌、腹直肌、阔筋膜张肌。

Muscles exercised: Gluteus maximus, the rectus femoris, the rectus abdominis, and the tensor fascia latae.

动作要领：

（1）单脚站立于平衡垫上，重心固定，上体直立，另一腿高抬，身体呈水平，骨盆中正。

（2）脚踩平衡垫，两腿呈 90°，上体正直，两手平举。（图 4-1-4）

Behavioral essentials:

(1) Standing on a balance pad with one foot,the center of gravity is fixed, the upper body is upright. Raise one of your legs while maintaining your body is horizontal and keeping your pelvis is in the middle.

(2) Step on the balance pad with your feet at a 90 degree angle, keep your upper body upright, and lift your hands flat. (Fig.4-1-4)

负荷强度：4 组，每组 15 秒，每组间歇 15 秒。

Intensity: 4 sets in all, each set for 15 seconds, then taking a 15-second break.

注意事项：

（1）在水平面内，膝关节不要超过脚尖。

（2）身体摆正，核心收紧。

Attentions:

(1) The knee should not exceed the tip of the foot in the horizontal plane.

(2) Straighten your body and tighten your core.

图 4-1-4 飞鸟支撑

Fig.4-1-4 Supporting the body like a flying bird

5. 平衡控腹 Balancing Your Abdomen

锻炼部位：股直肌、腹直肌。

Muscles exercised: Rectus femoris and rectus abdominis.

动作要领：

（1）仰卧地面，两手置于体侧，控制身体平衡，两脚并拢，屈膝或直腿均可。

（2）收腹，上身与大腿呈 90°，臀部坐在平衡垫上，身体呈“V”字形。

（3）注意力集中在腹部，注意呼吸。（图 4-1-5）

Behavioral essentials:

(1) Sit on the back with both hands on the side of your body to control the balance, bend the feet closely to each other or straight legs, both choices are ok.

(2) Keep the abdomen-contracting, and the angle between your upper body and the thigh should be right-angle, let your hip sit on the balance pad, and control the body in the shape of“V”.

(3) Focus on the abdomen and pay attention to breathing. (Fig.4-1-5)

负荷强度：4 组，每组 15 次，每组间歇 15 秒。

Intensity: 4 sets in all, each set for 15 times, then taking a 15-second break.

注意事项：

使臀部坐于平衡垫上，双腿抬起与地面间距为5～10厘米，躯干保持伸直，双臂在两侧保持平衡。

Attentions:

Sit with your hip on a balance pad, legs are raised 5-10 centimeter from the ground, torso keeps straight, arms are balanced on both sides.

图 4–1–5　平衡控腹
Fig.4–1–5　Balancing your abdomen

6. 平衡盘两头起 Balance Plate V-up

锻炼部位：腹直肌、腹横肌、腹斜肌、髋部屈肌。

Muscles exercised: Rectus abdominis, musculus trasversus abdominis, oblique abdominis, hip flexors.

动作要领：

（1）仰卧，两手伸直置于头顶以控制身体平衡，双腿高抬，上体屈曲。

（2）直臂前摆收腹，背部挺直，保持身体平衡，平衡垫置于腰部。（图 4-1-6）

Behavioral essentials:

(1) Lie on your back，extend your arms overhead for balance, raise your legs and bend your upper body.

(2) Lie with your waist on the balance pad. Hold your stomach in as you stretch arms and swing forward. Keep your back straight and your body balance. (Fig.4-1-6)

负荷强度：4组，每组15次，每组间歇15秒。

Intensity: 4 sets in all, each set for 15 times, then taking a 15- second break.

注意事项：

（1）背部不要弯曲，上身保持稳定。

（2）腰腹发力，伸臂前摆。

Attentions:

(1) Don't bend your back, keep your upper body steady.

(2) Lumbar abdomen to extend and arm forward swing.

图 4–1–6　平衡盘两头起
Fig.4–1–6　Balance plate V–up

7. 仰卧交叉 Supine Cross

锻炼部位：股直肌、腹直肌。

Muscles exercised: Rectus femoris and rectus abdominis.

动作要领：

（1）仰卧地面，两手置于体侧，控制身体平衡，两脚并拢，屈膝或直腿均可。

（2）收腹，上身与大腿呈 90°，臀部着地，身体呈“V”字形，转动腰部。

（3）注意力集中在腹部，注意呼吸，双手持平衡垫转动，自腰部至臀下。（图 4-1-7）

Behavioral essentials:

(1) Lie with your back on the floor. Place your hands on the side of the body to control your balance, bend your knees and put your feet together or just keep your legs straight.

(2) Hold your stomach in and the angle between your upper body and the thigh should be right-angle. Keep your hips on the floor and your body in a V-shape, and then twist your waist.

(3) Focus on your abdomen and breathing. Grasp the balance pad in both hands and twist your waist. (Fig.4-1-7)

负荷强度：4 组，每组 15 次，每组间歇 15 秒。

Intensity: 4 sets in all, each set for 15 times, then taking a 15-second break.

注意事项：

（1）双肩左右旋转。

（2）收紧腹部。

（3）臀部上侧支撑。

Attentions:

(1) Turn the shoulders left and right.

(2) Tighten your abdomen.

(3) Upper hip support.

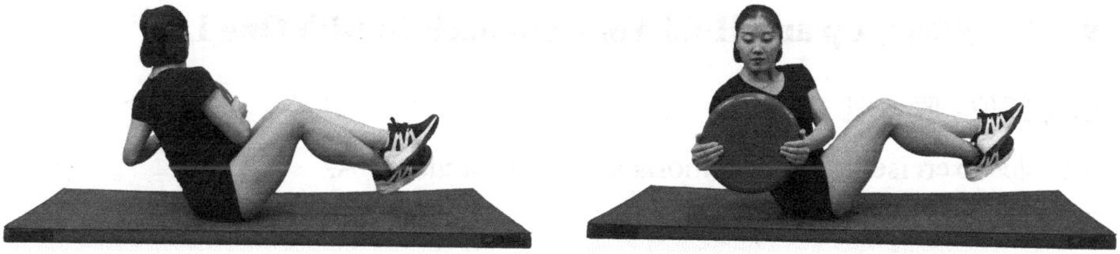

图 4-1-7 仰卧交叉

Fig.4-1-7 Supine cross

8. 腿夹平衡垫两头起 Leg Clamp Balance Pad V-up

锻炼部位：股直肌、腹直肌。

Muscles exercised: Rectus femoris and rectus abdominis.

动作要领：

（1）仰卧地面，两手伸直置于头顶以控制身体平衡，两脚并拢。

（2）平躺后，收腹，使手脚相碰，平衡垫放于两脚中间夹紧，或放于臀下。

（3）注意力集中在腹部，注意呼吸。（图 4-1-8）

Behavioral essentials:

(1) Lie with your back on the floor,extend your arms over head for balance and put your feet together.

(2) After lying on your back, hold your stomach in and bring your hands to meet feet. Squeeze the balance pad between or put it under your hips.

(3) Focus on your abdomen and pay attention to your breathing. (Fig.4-1-8)

负荷强度：4 组，每组 15 次，每组间歇 15 秒。

Intensity: 4 sets in all, each set for 15 times, then taking a 15-second break.

注意事项：

（1）抬腿至 90° ，手脚触碰。

（2）腰部贴地。

Attentions:

(1) Lift your leg to 90 degrees with your hands touching feet.

(2) The waist is attached to the ground.

图 4-1-8　腿夹平衡垫两头起

Fig.4-1-8　Leg clamp balance pad V-up

9. 单腿收腹起 Up and Hold Your Stomach In with One Leg

锻炼部位：股直肌、腹直肌。

Muscles exercised: Rectus femoris and rectus abdominis.

动作要领：

（1）仰卧，两手置于身体两侧以控制身体平衡。

（2）直腿，抬手臂收腹，使手脚相碰，后缓慢还原。

（3）注意力集中在腹部，注意呼吸，平衡垫放在腰部下面。（图 4-1-9）

Behavioral essentials:

(1) Lie on your back and place your hands on the side of the body to control your balance.

(2) Keep your legs straight and tuck in your stomach as you lift arms so that hands and feet can touch each other. Then restore your posture slowly.

(3) Focus on your abdomen and pay attention to your breathing. Put the balance pad under your waist. (Fig.4-1-9)

负荷强度：3 组，每组 15 次，每组间歇 15 秒。

Intensity: 3 sets in all, each set for 15 times, then taking a 15-second break.

注意事项：

（1）抬腿至 90°，手脚触碰。

（2）腰部贴地。

（3）另一条腿放松。

Attentions:

(1) Lift your leg to 90 degrees with your hands touching feet.

(2) The waist is attached to the ground.

(3) Relax your other leg.

图 4–1–9　单腿收腹起

Fig.4–1–9　Up and hold your stomach in with one leg

10. 仰卧双腿顶髋 Supination with Legs Against Hips

锻炼部位：腹直肌、股直肌、髂腰肌。

Muscles exercised: Rectus femoris, rectus abdominis and iliopsoas.

动作要领：

（1）仰卧，两手分开置于体侧，屈膝，大小腿呈 90°。

（2）平衡垫放于脚下，上体放松，腹部控制平衡，顶髋幅度要大。（图 4-1-10）

Behavioral essentials:

(1) Lie on your back and put your hands on the side of the body. Bend your knees until your thighs and calves can form a 90 degree angle.

(2) Place the balance pad under your feet and relax your torso. Use your abdomen control the balance and the action of against your hips should be obvious. (Fig.4-1-10)

负荷强度：3 组，每组 15 次，每组间歇 15 秒。

Intensity: 3 sets in all, each set for 15 times, then taking a 15-second break.

注意事项：

（1）腰部贴地，脚跟踩地。

（2）收腹，收紧臀部，不要过度挺腰，导致腰部发力感觉明显。

Attentions:

(1) The waist is attached to the ground and heel down.

(2) Strengthen your abdomen, tighten buttocks, do not extend the waist excessively. Feel the waist exertion obviously.

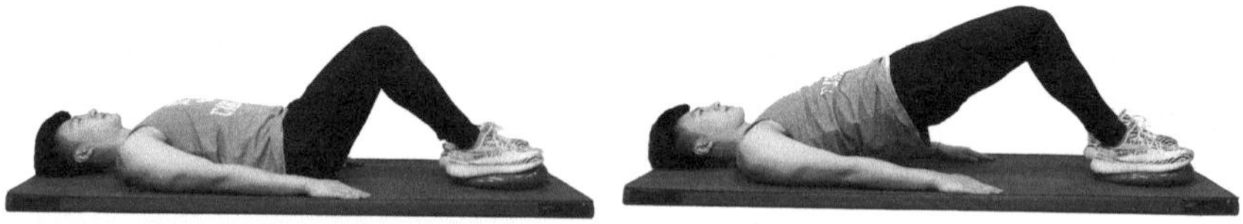

图 4-1-10　仰卧双腿顶髋

Fig.4-1-10　Supination with legs against hips

11. 仰卧单腿顶髋 Supination with One Leg Against Hips

锻炼部位：半腱肌、半膜肌、股二头肌。

Muscles exercised: Semitendinosus, semimembranosus and biceps femoris.

动作要领：

（1）水平仰卧，两手分开置于体侧，屈膝，大小腿呈 90° 弯曲。

（2）平衡垫放于脚下，上体放松，腹部控制平衡，顶髋幅度要大。（图 4-1-11）

Behavioral essentials:

(1) Lie horizontally on your back, place your hands apart on your sides, bend your knees, and bend your legs at a 90 degree angle.

(2) Put the balance pad under your foot and relax your torso. Use your abdomen control the balance and the action of against your hips should be obvious. (Fig.4-1-11)

负荷强度：4 组，每组 15 次，每组间歇 15 秒。

Intensity: 4 sets in all, each set for 15 times, then taking a 15-second break.

注意事项：

（1）腰部贴地，脚跟踩地。

（2）收腹，收紧臀部，不要过度挺腰，导致腰部发力感觉明显。

（3）在一条腿顶髋发力时，另一条腿直腿上抬，放松。

Attentions:

(1) The waist is attached to the ground and heel down.

(2) Strengthen your abdomen, tighten buttocks, do not extend the waist excessively. Feel the waist exertion obviously.

(3) When one leg exerts force on the hip, lift the other leg up straight and relax.

图 4-1-11 仰卧单腿顶髋
Fig.4-1-11 Supination with one leg against hips

12. 俯卧撑控肩 Push-ups

锻炼部位： 腹直肌、腹外斜肌、腹内斜肌、髂腰肌、臀大肌、股二头肌。

Muscles exercised: Rectus femoris, external oblique, internal oblique, iliopsoas, gluteus maximus and biceps femoris.

动作要领：

（1）两脚并拢，两手分开与肩同宽，四肢跪式支撑，背部挺直，脚尖着地。

（2）眼睛平视前方，平衡垫放于手掌下方。（图 4-1-12）

Behavioral essentials:

(1) Close your feet together and put your hands apart as wide as a shoulder's distance apart. The four limbs support the body with the back tight and only the toes on the ground.

(2) Keep your eyes looking straight ahead and put the balance pad under your palms. (Fig.4-1-12)

负荷强度： 4 组，每组 15 次，每组间歇 15 秒。

Intensity: 4 sets in all, each set for 15 times, then taking a 15-second break.

注意事项：

（1）保持核心收紧，身体不要晃动。

（2）臀部不能坍塌。

Attentions:

(1) Keep the core tight and body steady.

(2) The hip can't go down.

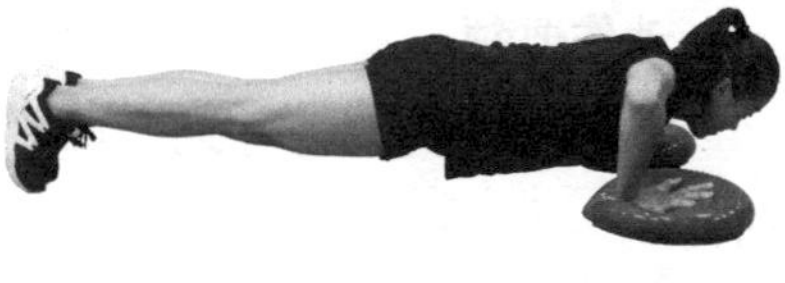

图 4-1-12 俯卧撑控肩
Fig.4-1-12 Push-ups

13. 核心平板支撑 Core Plank

锻炼部位： 腹直肌、腹外斜肌、腹内斜肌、髂腰肌、臀大肌、股二头肌。

Muscles exercised: Rectus femoris, external oblique, internal oblique, iliopsoas, gluteus maximus and biceps femoris.

动作要领：

（1）俯卧，两脚并拢，两手分开与肩同宽，双肘支撑地面，背部挺直。

（2）腹部和髋部紧张，肘部保持平衡，平衡垫置于肘关节下方。（图 4-1-13）

Behavioral essentials:

(1) Come into a prone position with your feet close together and your hands as wide as a shoulder's distance apart. Support your body with elbows on the ground and keep your back tight.

(2) Tighten your abdomen and hips, keep your elbows balanced, and place the balance pad under your elbows. (Fig.4-1-13)

负荷强度：4 组，每组 15 次，每组间歇 15 秒。

Intensity: 4 sets in all, each set for 15 times, then taking a 15-second break.

注意事项：

（1）撑起时背部不能弯曲，身体保持成一条直线。

（2）颈部不要下垂，头部保持自然位置。

Attentions:

(1) Don't bend your back when you prop it up. Keep your body in a straight line.

(2) Do not drop your neck, keep your head in natural position.

图 4-1-13　核心平板支撑
Fig.4-1-13　Core plank

14. 单臂平板支撑 One-arm Plank

锻炼部位：腹直肌、腹外斜肌、腹内斜肌、髂腰肌、臀大肌、股二头肌。

Muscles exercised: Rectus femoris, external oblique, internal oblique, iliopsoas, gluteus maximus and biceps femoris.

动作要领：

（1）俯卧，两脚并拢，两手分开与肩同宽，一臂单肘支撑地面，另一臂向前伸。

（2）背部挺直，腹部和髋部紧张，肘部保持平衡，平衡垫置于肘关节下方。（图 4-1-14）

Behavioral essentials:

(1) Come into a prone position with your feet close together and your hands as wide as a shoulder's distance apart. Support your body with one elbow on the ground and extend the other forward.

(2) Keep your back straight, tighten your abdomen and hips, keep your elbows balanced, and place the balance pad under your elbows. (Fig.4-1-14)

负荷强度：4 组，每组 20 次，每组间歇 15 秒。

Intensity: 4 sets in all, each set for 20 times, then taking a 15-second break.

注意事项：

（1）动作进行时，背部挺直，身体保持成一条直线。

（2）伸臂后保持动作 1～2 秒再还原。

Attentions:

(1) Keep your back straight and keep your body in a straight line.

(2) After the arm extension maintain movement 1-2 seconds before recovery.

图 4-1-14　单臂平板支撑
Fig.4-1-14　One-arm plank

15. 侧卧肘支撑 Side Elbow Support

锻炼部位：腹直肌、腹外斜肌、腹内斜肌、髂腰肌、臀大肌、股二头肌。

Muscles exercised: Rectus femoris, external oblique, internal oblique, iliopsoas, gluteus maximus and biceps femoris.

动作要领：

（1）侧卧，两脚并拢，一臂肘关节支撑地面，另一臂上举，背部挺直。

（2）腹部和髋部紧张，肘部保持平衡，平衡垫置于肘关节下方。（图 4-1-15）

Behavioral essentials:

(1) Lie on your side with the feet close together. Keep your back straight, put one elbow on the ground and extend the other toward the ceiling.

(2) Tighten your abdomen and hips, keep your elbows balanced, and place the balance pad under your elbows. (Fig.4-1-15)

负荷强度：3 组，每组 15 次，每组间歇 15 秒。

Intensity: 3 sets in all, each set for 15 times, then taking a 15-second break.

注意事项：

（1）保持上身稳定，腰部不要弯曲。

（2）身体成一条直线。

图 4-1-15　侧卧肘支撑
Fig.4-1-15　Side elbow support

Attentions:

(1) Keep your upper body steady and don't bend your waist.

(2) Keep your body in a straight line.

16. 侧卧肘支撑抬腿 Leg-lifting with Side Elbow Support

锻炼部位：腹直肌、腹外斜肌、腹内斜肌、髂腰肌、臀大肌。

Muscles exercised: Rectus femoris, external oblique, internal oblique, iliopsoas and gluteus maximus.

动作要领：

（1）侧卧，两脚并拢，一臂肘关节支撑地面，另一臂上举，背部挺直，向上抬起一条腿。

（2）腹部和髋部紧张，肘部保持平衡，平衡垫置于肘关节下方。（图 4-1-16）

Behavioral essentials:

(1) Lie on your side with the feet close together. Put one elbow on the ground and extend the other toward the ceiling. Keep your back straight and extend one of your legs.

(2) Tighten your abdomen and hips, keep your elbows balanced, and place the balance pad under your elbows. (Fig.4-1-16)

负荷强度：4 组，每组 20 次，每组间歇 15 秒。

Intensity: 4 sets in all, each set for 20 times, then taking a 15-second break.

注意事项：

（1）抬腿后保持几秒后放下，不能使用惯性完成下一个抬腿动作。

（2）保持上身稳定，腰部不要弯曲。

Attentions:

(1) Hold the action slightly. Do not use inertia to complete the next move.

(2) Keep your upper body steady and don't bend your waist.

图 4–1–16　侧卧肘支撑抬腿

Fig.4–1–16　Leg–lifting with side elbow support

17. 侧卧肘支撑前后摆腿 Swing Legs Forward and Backward with Side Elbow Support

锻炼部位：腹直肌、腹外斜肌、腹内斜肌、髂腰肌、臀大肌。

Muscles exercised: Rectus femoris, external oblique, internal oblique, iliopsoas and gluteus maximus.

动作要领：

（1）侧卧，两脚并拢，一臂肘关节支撑地面，另一臂上举，背部挺直，向上抬起一腿，前后摆动。

（2）腹部和髋部紧张，肘部保持平衡，平衡垫置于肘关节下方。（图 4-1-17）

Behavioral essentials:

(1) Lie on your side with the feet close together. Put one elbow on the ground and extend the other toward the ceiling. Keep your back straight and extend one of your legs then swing it forward and backward.

(2) Tighten your abdomen and hips, keep your elbows balanced, and place the balance pad under your elbows. (Fig.4-1-17)

负荷强度：4 组，每组 15 次，每组间歇 15 秒。

Intensity: 4 sets in all, each set for 15 times, then taking a 15-second break.

注意事项：

（1）动作张开后稍微保持，不能使用惯性完成下一个动作。

（2）上身保持挺直，不能弯曲。

Attentions:

(1) Hold the action slightly. Do not use inertia to complete the next move.

(2) Keep your upper body steady and don't bend.

图 4–1–17　侧卧肘支撑前后摆腿
Fig.4–1–17　Swing legs forward and backward with side elbow support

18. 侧卧肘支撑转体 Twist with Side Elbow Support

锻炼部位：腹直肌、腹外斜肌、腹内斜肌、髂腰肌、臀大肌。

Muscles exercised: Rectus femoris, external oblique abdominis, internal oblique abdominis, iliopsoas and gluteus maximus.

动作要领：

（1）侧卧，两脚并拢，一臂支撑地面，另一臂上举，背部挺直，转动肩部带动身体转动，上举的手臂摆动于腰下。

（2）收紧腹部和髋部，肘部保持平衡，平衡垫置于肘关节下方。（图 4-1-18）

Behavioral essentials:

(1) Lie on your side with your feet close together. Put one elbow on the ground and extend the other arm toward the ceiling. Keep your back straight, rotate your shoulder to turn the torso, and let your raised arm swing under your waist.

(2) Tighten your abdomen and hips, keep your elbows balanced, and place the balance pad under your elbows. (Fig.4-1-18)

负荷强度：4 组，每组 15 次，每组间歇 15 秒。

Intensity: 4 sets in all, each set for 15 times, then taking a 15-second break.

注意事项：

（1）动作张开后稍微保持，不能使用惯性完成下一个动作。

（2）转体过程中上身保持挺直，不能弯曲。

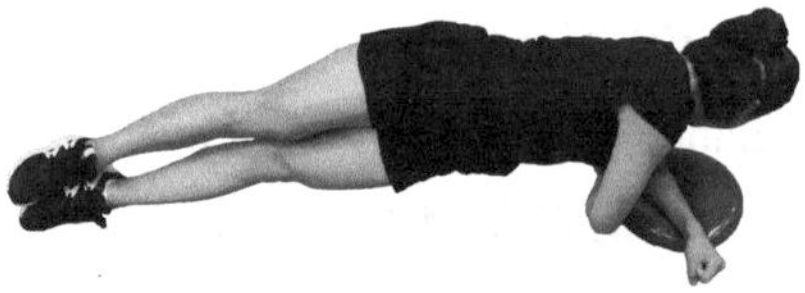

图 4-1-18　侧卧肘支撑转体

Fig.4-1-18　Twist with side elbow support

Attentions:

(1) Hold the position briefly. Don't use inertia to complete the next move.

(2) Keep your upper body steady and don't bend when you twist.

19. 单腿平板支撑 One-leg Plank

锻炼部位：腹直肌、腹外斜肌、腹内斜肌、髂腰肌、臀大肌。

Muscles exercised: Rectus femoris, external oblique abdominis, internal oblique abdominis, iliopsoas and gluteus maximus.

动作要领：

（1）俯卧，两脚上下分开，两臂屈肘与肩同宽，双肘支撑地面，背部挺直。

（2）收紧腹部和髋部，肘部保持平衡，平衡垫置于肘关节下方。（图 4-1-19）

Behavioral essentials:

(1) Come into a prone position and lift one of your legs, then bend your elbows with your arms shoulder-width apart, rest your elbows on the ground, and keep your back straight.

(2) Tighten your abdomen and hips, keep your elbows stable, and place the balance pad under your elbows. (Fig.4-1-19)

负荷强度：4 组，每组 20 次，每组间歇 15 秒。

Intensity: 4 sets in all, each set for 20 times, then taking a 15-second break.

注意事项：

（1）撑起时背部不能弯曲，保持一条直线。

（2）脚尖发力支撑。

Attentions:

(1) Don't bend your back when you support your body. Keep your body in a straight line.

(2) Use toes to support.

图 4-1-19 单腿平板支撑
Fig.4-1-19 One-leg Plank

20. 俯卧背起 Prone Up

锻炼部位：腹直肌、腹外斜肌、腹内斜肌、髂腰肌、臀大肌。

Muscles exercised: Rectus femoris, external oblique abdominis, internal oblique abdominis, iliopsoas and gluteus maximus.

动作要领：

（1）俯卧，双手交叉固定于腰部。

（2）背起至大幅度。手脚同时背起，平衡垫置于腹部下方，注意保持平衡。（图 4-1-20）

Behavioral essentials:

(1) Lie on your stomach and place your hands across your waist.

(2) Back up to a large extent, put your hands and feet back up together. Place the balance pad under your abdomen to keep balance. (Fig.4-1-20)

负荷强度：4 组，每组 20 次，每组间歇 15 秒。

Intensity: 4 sets in all, each set for 20 times, then taking a 15-second break.

注意事项：

（1）双腿尽量向上抬，保证锻炼质量。

（2）动作进行时颈部保持固定，不要随意摆动。

Attentions:

(1) Keep your legs as high as possible to ensure quality.

(2) Keep your neck fixed and don't move unnecessarily.

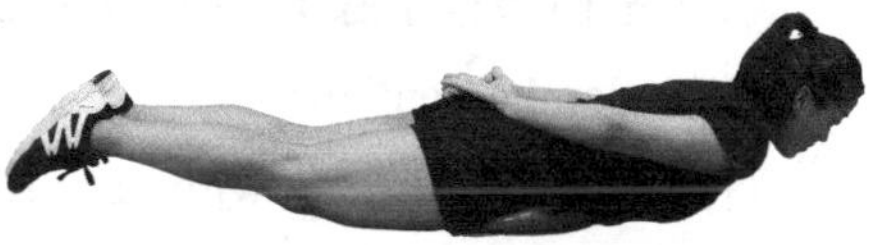

图 4-1-20 俯卧背起
Fig.4-1-20 Prone up

21. 跪桥抬腿 Single Leg Lift in Kneeling Bridge

锻炼部位：背阔肌、臀大肌、竖脊肌。

Muscles exercised: Latissimus dorsi, gluteus maximus and erector spinae.

动作要领：

（1）跪姿，双手与肩同宽撑于地面，一膝跪式支撑，另一腿伸直向后摆。

（2）平衡垫置于支撑膝下方。（图 4-1-21）

Behavioral Essentials:

(1) Kneel on all fours with your hands shoulder-width apart and put them on the ground, and one leg knee to support, the other straight backswing.

(2) Put the balance pad under your knees. (Fig.4-1-21)

负荷强度：4 组，每组 15 次，每组间歇 15 秒。

Intensity: 4 sets in all, each set for 15 times, then taking a 15-second break.

注意事项：

（1）上体保持挺直，不能弯曲。

（2）后摆过程中腿部尽量伸直，不要弯曲。

Attentions:

(1) Keep your upper body straight and don't bend.

(2) Try to keep your legs straight and don't bend when swinging back.

图 4-1-21　跪桥抬腿

Fig.4-1-21　Single leg lift in kneeling bridge

22. 跪桥单手单腿支撑 Kneeling Bridge with one Hand and One Leg

锻炼部位：背阔肌、臀大肌、竖脊肌。

Muscles exercised: Latissimus dorsi, gluteus maximus and erector spinae.

动作要领：

（1）跪姿，右手撑于地面，左手抬起，左膝跪地支撑，右腿伸直向后摆。

（2）平衡垫置于膝下。（图 4-1-22）

Behavioral essentials:

(1) Kneel on all fours with your right hand on the ground and raise your left hand. Keep your left leg knee to support, the other straight backswing.

(2) Put the balance pad under your knees. (Fig.4-1-22)

负荷强度：4 组，每组 15 次，每组间歇 15 秒。

Intensity: 4 sets in all, each set for 15 times, then taking a 15-second break.

注意事项：

（1）上体保持挺直，不能弯曲。

（2）颈部保持固定，不要随意摆动。

Attentions:

(1) Keep your upper body straight and don't bend.

(2) Keep your neck fixed and don't move at will.

图 4-1-22　跪桥单手单腿支撑

Fig.4-1-22　Kneeling bridge with one hand and one leg

第二节　哑铃、杠铃训练

Section 2　Dumbbell and Barbell Training

1. 哑铃侧蹲 Dumbbell Side Squat

锻炼部位：股直肌、臀大肌。

Muscles exercised: Rectus femoris and ectogluteus.

动作要领：

（1）双脚开立，距离为肩宽的两倍，双手握住哑铃贴近胸口。

（2）臀部向一侧后坐，膝关节与脚尖方向一致。

（3）臀部发力蹲起到站立位置。

（4）下蹲时吸气，站起时呼气。（图 4-2-1）

Behavioral essentials:

(1) Stand with your feet apart , make them twice times as wide as your shoulder's distance apart and hold the dumbbells close to your chest with both hands.

(2) The hips sit back to one side with the knees facing the toes.

(3) Stand up by the force of the hips.

(4) In hale when you squat down and exhale when you stand up. (Fig.4-2-1)

负荷强度：2 组，每组 20 次，每组间歇 10 秒。

Intensity: 2 sets in all, each set for 20 times, then taking a 10-second break.

注意事项：

（1）腹部核心收紧。

（2）臀部向后坐。

Attentions:

(1) Tighten the core muscles of the abdomen.

(2) Let your hips squat backward.

图 4–2–1 哑铃侧蹲

Fig.4–2–1 Dumbbell side squat

2. 哑铃侧平举 Dumbbells Lateral Raise

锻炼部位：竖脊肌、腹外斜肌。

Muscles exercised: Erector spinae and obliquus externus abdominis.

动作要领：

（1）双手持哑铃下垂，以肩部为轴，缓缓侧平举。

（2）下放时双臂缓慢向内侧合拢。

（3）平举时呼气，下放时吸气。（图 4-2-2）

Behavioral essentials:

(1) Hold dumbbells with both hands and hang them down, using the shoulders as the axis and slowly lift the dumbbells horizontally.

(2) Your arms are slowly closing in when you lower the dumbbells.

(3) Exhale when lifting, inhale when lowering. (Fig.4-2-2)

负荷强度：2 组，每组 15 次，每组间歇 10 秒。

Intensity: 2 sets in all, each set for 15 times, then taking a 10-second break.

注意事项：

（1）双肩下沉，绷紧手臂。

（2）手肘微屈。

Attentions:

(1) Keep your shoulders down and tighten the arms.

(2) Bent elbows slightly.

图 4-2-2 哑铃侧平举

Fig.4-2-2 Dumbbells Lateral Raise

3. 哑铃卧推 Dumbbells Bench Press

锻炼部位： 腹直肌。

Muscles exercised: Rectus abdominis.

动作要领：

（1）仰卧于功能凳，臀部收紧。

（2）双手持哑铃上举。

（3）上举时要胸部先发力，上臂向中间靠拢。

（4）上举时呼气，下落时吸气。（图 4-2-3）

Behavioral essentials:

(1) Lying supine on the functional bench, with your hips tightened.

(2) Push dumbbells upwards with both hands.

(3) When pushing up, start with the chest and bring your upper arm closer to the center.

(4) Exhale when pushing up and inhale when lowering. (Fig.4-2-3)

负荷强度： 2 组，每组 20 次，每组间歇 8 秒。

Intensity: 2 sets in all, each set for 20 times, then taking a 8-second break.

注意事项：

（1）腹部收紧。

（2）胸部收紧。

Attentions:

(1) Keep your abdominal tight.

(2) Tighten your chest.

图 4-2-3 哑铃卧推
Fig.4-2-3 Dumbbells Bench press

4. 哑铃臂前伸 Dumbbells Arm Extends Forward

锻炼部位：腹外斜肌、竖脊肌。

Muscles exercised: External oblique and erector spinae.

动作要领：

（1）绷紧肩关节，保持身体稳定。

（2）缓慢将哑铃水平向前伸出、向后收回。（图 4-2-4）

Behavioral essentials:

(1) Tighten the shoulder joint and keep the body stability.

(2) Slowly extend the dumbbells horizontally forward and retract them. (Fig.4-2-4)

负荷强度：2 组，每组 20 次，每组间歇 10 秒。

Intensity: 2 sets in all, each set for 20 times, then taking a 10-second break.

注意事项：

（1）哑铃水平向前伸出。

（2）肱二头肌有明显发力。

Attentions:

(1) Extend the dumbbells horizontally forward.

(2) Use the power of the biceps brachium.

图 4-2-4 哑铃臂前伸
Fig.4-2-4 Dumbbells arm extends forward

5. 哑铃硬拉 Dumbbell Deadlift

锻炼部位：腹直肌。

Muscles exercised: Rectus abdominis.

动作要领：

（1）哑铃运动轨迹始终贴近身体。

（2）保持腰背挺直，腹部核心收紧。

（3）站起时呼气，俯身时吸气。（图 4-2-5）

Behavioral essentials:

(1) The track of the dumbbell is always close to the body.

(2) Keep your back straight and tighten your core muscles of the abdomen.

(3) Exhale when you stand up and inhale when you lean over. (Fig.4-2-5)

负荷强度：2 组，每组 15 次，每组间歇 15 秒。

Intensity: 2 sets in all, each set for 15 times, then taking a 15-second break.

注意事项：

（1）不要耸肩。

（2）臀部发力站起。

Attentions:

(1) Don't shrug.

(2) Stand up by the force of the hips.

图 4-2-5 哑铃硬拉

Fig.4-2-5 Dumbbell deadlift

6. 哑铃 8 字划圈 Use Dumbbell Make Circles in Shape of 8

锻炼部位：斜方肌、腹横肌。

Muscles exercised: Cucullaris and transverse muscle of abdomen.

动作要领：

（1）肩胛骨夹紧并下沉。

（2）上半身收紧，保持不动。

（3）向外侧划圈呼气。（图 4-2-6）

Behavioral essentials:

(1) Tighten your scapula and lower them.

(2) Tighten your upper body and tight still.

(3) Exhale when drawing circles to the outside. (Fig.4-2-6)

负荷强度：2 组，每组 20 次，每组间歇 10 秒。

Intensity: 2 sets in all, each set for 20 times, then taking a 10-second break.

注意事项：

（1）抬起左肩划圈。

图 4-2-6 哑铃 8 字划圈

Fig.4-2-6 Use dumbbll make circles in shape of 8

（2）抬起右肩划圈。

Attentions:

(1) Lift the left shoulder to make a circle.

(2) Lift the right shoulder to make a circle.

7. 左腿哑铃箭步蹲 Left-leg Dumbbells Lunges

锻炼部位：股直肌、臀大肌。

Muscles exercised: Rectus femoris and gluteus maximus.

动作要领：

（1）左腿在前，右脚脚尖点地支撑。

（2）双手握着哑铃在身体两侧。

（3）左腿、左脚跟发力蹲起至站立姿势。（图 4-2-7）

Behavioral essentials:

(1) The left leg is in front and the toe of the right foot touches the ground.

(2) Hold the dumbbells in both hands and put your hands on the both sides of the body.

(3) Stand up by the force of left leg and left heel. (Fig.4-2-7)

负荷强度：2 组，每组 25 次，每组间歇 12 秒。

Intensity: 2 sets in all, each set for 25 times, then taking a 12-second break.

图 4–2–7　左腿哑铃箭步蹲

Fig.4–2–7　Left–leg dumbbells lunges

注意事项：

（1）脚跟发力。

（2）竖直蹲起。

（3）脚尖点地支撑。

Attentions:

(1) Exert power of heel.

(2) Squat and rise vertically.

(3) Support the leg with the toe on the ground.

8. 右腿哑铃箭步蹲 Right-leg Dumbbells Lunges

锻炼部位：臀大肌、股直肌。

Muscles exercised: Gluteus maximus and rectus femoris.

动作要领：

（1）右腿在前，左脚脚尖点地支撑。

（2）膝关节弯曲。

（3）右腿、右脚跟发力蹲起至站立姿势。（图 4-2-8）

Behavioral essentials:

(1) The right leg is in front and the toe of the left foot touches the ground.

(2) Bend your knees.

(3) Stand up by the force of right leg and right heel. (Fig.4-2-8)

负荷强度：2 组，每组 25 次，每组间歇 10 秒。

Intensity: 2 sets in all, each set for 25 times, then taking a 10-second break.

注意事项：

（1）腹部收紧。

（2）肩膀后缩下沉。

Attentions:

(1) Tighten the abdomen.

(2) Retract and lower your shoulders.

图 4-2-8　右腿哑铃箭步蹲

Fig.4-2-8　Right-leg dumbbells lunges

9. 上斜哑铃飞鸟 Incline Dumbbells Fly

锻炼部位：竖脊肌。

Muscles exercised: Erector spinae.

动作要领：

（1）将训练凳的角度调整为约 30°　。

（2）外旋手臂，举起哑铃在身体两侧。

（3）肩膀始终后缩下沉。（图 4-2-9）

Behavioral essentials:

(1) The angle of the training bench is about 30° .

(2) Rotate your arms and lift the dumbbells to the both sides of your body.

(3) Retract and lower your shoulders. (Fig.4-2-9)

负荷强度：2 组，每组 20 次，每组间歇 10 秒。

Intensity: 2 sets in all, each set for 20 times, then taking a 10-second break.

注意事项：

（1）腹部收紧。

（2）手肘稍低于肩膀。

（3）掌心微微朝内。

Attentions:

(1) Tighten your abd-omen.

(2) The elbow is slightly lower than your shoulder.

(3) The palm is slightly inward.

图 4–2–9　上斜哑铃飞鸟

Fig.4–2–9　Incline dumbbells fly

10. 哑铃钻石卧推 Dumbbell Diamond Bench Press

锻炼部位：竖脊肌、腹斜肌。

Muscles exercised: Erector spinae and the oblique muscles.

动作要领：

（1）手臂紧贴身体两侧。

（2）肩胛骨后缩下沉，腰部微微离地。（图 4-2-10）

Behavioral essentials:

(1) Keep your arms close to the both sides of your body.

(2) Retract the scapula and make the waist slightly off the ground. (Fig.4-2-10)

负荷强度：2 组，每组 20 次，每组间歇 10 秒。

Intensity: 2 sets in all, each set for 20 times, then taking a 10-second break.

注意事项：

（1）腹部收紧，腰部微微离地。

（2）上臂贴近身体。

Attentions:

(1) Tighten the abdomen and make the waist slightly off the ground.

(2) Keep yourupper arm close to your body.

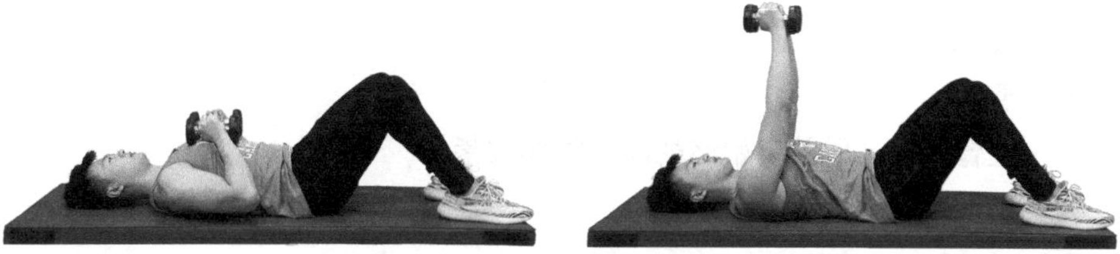

图 4-2-10　哑铃钻石卧推
Fig.4-2-10　Dumbbell diamond bench press

11. 哑铃反握划船 Dumbbell Reverse Grasp Row

锻炼部位：竖脊肌、腹直肌。

Muscles exercised: Erector spinae and rectus abdominis.

动作要领：

（1）掌心朝前，反握哑铃。

（2）挺直背部俯身 70°　。

（3）前臂垂直于地面。（图 4-2-11）

Behavioral essentials:

(1) Reverse hold the dumbbells with palms facing forward.

(2) Keep your back straight and bent over 70°　.

(3) The forearm is perpendicular to the ground. (Fig.4-2-11)

负荷强度：2 组，每组 20 次，每组间歇 8 秒。

Intensity: 2 sets in all, each set for 20 times, then taking a 8-second break.

注意事项：

（1）掌心朝前。

（2）手肘紧贴身体两身侧。

（3）挺胸，背部完全挺直。

Attentions:

(1) The palms are facing forward.

(2) Keep your elbows close to the both sides of your body.

图 4-2-11　哑铃反握划船
Fig.4-2-11　Dumbbell reverse grasp row

(3) Chest out and keep your back completely straight.

12. 仰卧哑铃屈伸 Dumbbells Lying Extension

锻炼部位：腹直肌。

Muscles exercised: Rectus abdominis.

动作要领：

（1）上臂固定，肘关节始终朝前，腹部收紧。

（2）下放时控制速度。（图 4-2-12）

Behavioral essentials:

(1) Keep the upper arms fixed. The elbow joints are always facing forwards and the abdomen is tightened when contracting.

(2) Control your speed while lowering the dumbbell. (Fig.4-2-12)

负荷强度：2 组，每组 25 次，每组间歇 12 秒。

Intensity: 2 sets in all, each set for 25 times, then taking a 12-second break.

注意事项：

（1）腹部收紧。

（2）肘关节朝前。

Attentions:

(1) Tighten the abdomen.

(2) The elbow joints are facing forwards.

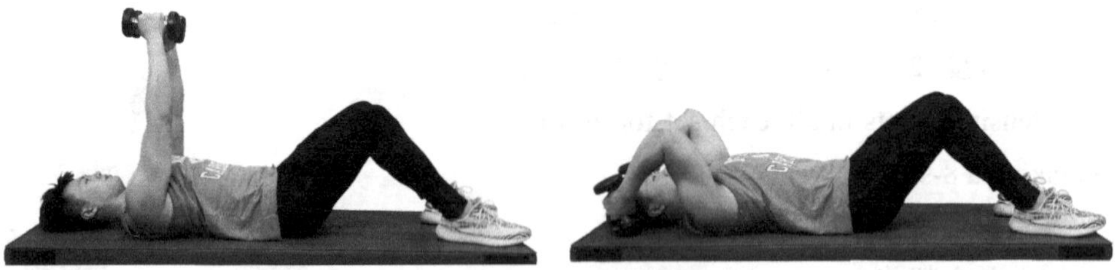

图 4-2-12 仰卧哑铃屈伸

Fig.4-2-12 Dumbbells lying extension

13. 哑铃坐姿推举 Dumbbells Seated Press

锻炼部位：竖脊肌。

Muscles exercised: Erector spinae.

动作要领：

（1）双脚踩实地面。

（2）肩膀后缩下沉，臀部、背部贴实靠背。

（3）前臂保持垂直于地面。（图 4-2-13）

Behavioral essentials:

(1) Keep your feet on the ground firmly.

(2) Retract and sink your shoulders with your back and hips firmly against the back of the seat.

(3) Keep the forearms perpendicular to the ground. (Fig.4-2-13)

负荷强度： 2 组，每组 30 次，每组间歇 10 秒。

Intensity: 2 sets in all, each set for 30 times, then taking a 10-second break.

注意事项：

（1）腹部收紧。

（2）臀部贴实凳子。

Attentions:

(1) Tighten your abdomen.

(2) Put your hips on the stool firmly.

图 4-2-13 哑铃坐姿推举

Fig.4-2-13 Dumbbells seated press

14. 哑铃后撤 Dumbbell Stepback

锻炼部位： 臀大肌、股直肌。

Muscles exercised: Gluteus maximus and rectus femoris.

动作要领：

（1）上半身挺直，哑铃置于身体两侧。

（2）下蹲时前侧大腿与身体呈 90° 。

（3）保持每次步幅大小相同。（图 4-2-14）

Behavioral essentials:

(1) Keep your upper body straight and hold the dumbbells at the both sides of your body.

(2) The front thigh is perpendicular to your body when squatting.

(3) Keep each stride is the same size.（图 4-2-14）

负荷强度： 2 组，每组 35 次，每组间歇 10 秒。

Intensity: 2 sets in all, each set for 35 times, then taking a 10-second break.

注意事项：

（1）腹部收紧，上身挺直。

（2）前腿膝关节呈 90° 。

Attentions:

(1) Tighten your abdomen and keep your upper body straight.

(2) The angle of the front leg' s knee joint will be 90° .

图 4-2-14　哑铃后撤

Fig.4-2-14　Dumbbell Stepback

15. 哑铃臀桥卧推 Dumbbells Hip Bridge Bench Press

锻炼部位：腹直肌、臀大肌。

Muscles exercised: Rectus abdominis and gluteus maximus.

动作要领：

（1）核心收紧，臀大肌发力保持静力臀桥。

（2）上背部支撑，肩胛骨后缩下沉。

（3）发力时上臂向身体中线靠近。（图 4-2-15）

Behavioral essentials:

(1) Tighten the core muscles and use the force of gluteus maximus to maintain a static gluteal bridge.

(2) The upper back supports the body and the scapula retracts and sinks.

(3) When exerting force, bring the upper arm closer to the midline of the body. (Fig.4-2-15)

负荷强度：2 组，每组 30 次，每组间歇 10 秒。

Intensity: 2 sets in all, each set for 30 times, then taking a 10-second break.

注意事项：

（1）核心收紧。

（2）肩胛骨后缩平贴地面。

（3）发力前上臂与上体呈 70° 左右。

Attentions:

(1) Tighten your core muscles.

(2) Retract the scapula and let it on the ground.

(3) Before exerting force, the upper arms are at an angle of about 70 degrees to your upper body.

图 4–2–15　哑铃臀桥卧推

Fig.4–2–15　Dumbbells hip bridge bench press

16. 宽握哑铃划船 Wide-grip Dumbbells Row

锻炼部位：竖脊肌、腹外斜肌。

Muscles exercised: Erector spinae and external oblique.

动作要领：

（1）下背部保持挺直，腰部收紧。

（2）下放时肩胛骨打开前伸。

（3）拉起时肩胛骨收紧后缩。（图 4-2-16）

Behavioral essentials:

(1) Keep the underpart of your back straight and tight your waist.

(2) Extend the scapula forward when you putting the dumbbell down.

(3) Keep the scapula tightened and retracted when you pulling the dumbbell up. (Fig.4-2-16)

负荷强度：2 组，每组 40 次，每组间

图 4–2–16　宽握哑铃划船

Fig.4–2–16　Wide–grip dumbbells row

歇 10 秒。

Intensity: 2 sets in all, each set for 40 times, then taking a 10-second break.

注意事项：

（1）腹部收紧，下背部挺直。

（2）肩胛骨前伸，背部展开。

Attentions:

(1) Tighten your abdomen and keep the underpart of your back straight.

(2) Keep the scapula extends forward and the expand your back.

17. 哑铃平地飞鸟 Dumbbells Ground Fly

锻炼部位：腹外斜肌、竖脊肌。

Muscles exercised: External oblique and erector spinae.

动作要领：

（1）肘关节微屈，腹部收紧。

（2）下放时控制速度。（图 4-2-17）

Behavioral essentials:

(1) Bend your elbows slightly and tighten your abdomen.

(2) Control your speed while lowering the dumbbell. (Fig.4-2-17)

负荷强度：2 组，每组 30 次，每组间歇 12 秒。

Intensity: 2 sets in all, each set for 30 times, then taking a 12-second break.

图 4-2-17　哑铃平地飞鸟

Fig.4-2-17　Dumbbells ground fly

注意事项：

（1）腹部收紧，腰部微离地。

（2）肘关节保持微屈。

Attentions:

(1) Tighten the abdomen and let the waist off the ground slightly.

(2) The elbow remains slightly bent.

18. 哑铃俄罗斯转体 Dumbbell Russian Twist

锻炼部位：腹外斜肌、腹直肌。

Muscles exercised: External oblique and rectus abdominis.

动作要领：

（1）转动双肩来带动手臂的移动。

（2）下背挺直，上背微弓起。（图 4-2-18）

Behavioral essentials:

(1) Turn around your shoulders to move your arms.

(2) Keep your lower back straight and your upper back slightly arching. (Fig.4-2-18)

负荷强度：2 组，每组 35 次，每组间歇 10 秒。

Intensity: 2 sets in all, each set for 35 times, then taking a 10-second break.

注意事项：

（1）哑铃触地。

（2）臀部上侧支撑地面。

（3）双腿保持固定。

Attentions:

(1) Let the dumbbell touch the ground.

(2) Let the upper part of your hips on the ground.

(3) Keep your legs fixed.

图 4–2–18　哑铃俄罗斯转体
Fig.4–2–18　Dumbbell Russian twist

19. 哑铃单臂划船 One-arm Dumbbell Row

锻炼部位：腹外斜肌。

Muscles exercised: External oblique.

动作要领：

（1）下背部保持挺直，腰部不要转动。

（2）下放时肩胛骨打开前伸。

（3）顶端保持 1～2 秒。（图 4-2-19）

Behavioral essentials:

(1) Keep the underpart of your back straight and don't twist your waist.

(2) Extend your scapula forward when putting down the dumbbell.

(3) Hold for 1 to 2 seconds when you pulling up the dumbbell to the top. (Fig.4-2-19)

负荷强度：2 组，每组 40 次，每组间歇 10 秒。

Intensity: 2 sets in all, each set for 40 times, then taking a 10-second break.

注意事项：

（1）肩胛骨前伸。

（2）颈椎保持中立位置。

Attentions:

(1) Stretch your shoulder blades forward.

(2) Keep the cervical spine in a neutral position.

图 4–2–19　哑铃单臂划船
Fig.4–2–19　One–arm dumbbell row

20. 杠铃颈前推举 Barbell Shoulder Press

锻炼部位：三角肌前束。

Muscles exercised: Deltoid anterior.

动作要领：

（1）选择自然站立时，两手握住横杠，握距比肩稍宽 2～5 厘米。

（2）选择坐姿时，选用 80°～85° 靠背的长凳，后背要完全靠在靠背上。

（3）提杠铃由体前至肩上，掌心向上。

（4）把杠铃贴脸部向上推起至两臂伸直在头顶上方，然后，慢慢循原路放至肩上。（图 4-2-20）

Behavioral essentials:

(1) When choosing to stand naturally, hold the horizontal bar with both hands, with a grip distance slightly wider than your shoulders by 2-5 centimeters.

(2) When choosing a sitting posture, use a bench with an 80°-85° backrest, with

the back fully resting on the backrest.

(3) Lift the barbell from the front of your body to your shoulders, with your palms facing upwards.

(4) Push the barbell up against your face until your arms are straight above your head, then slowly lower it down to your shoulders along the same path. (Fig.4-2-20)

负荷强度：3 组，每组 12 次，每组间歇 20 秒。

Intensity: 3 sets in all, each set for 12 times, then taking a 20-second break.

注意事项：

（1）动作开始时，肩关节保持稳定，身体不要晃动。

（2）进行推举时，腰部注意不要过于向前躬，尽量保持躯干直立。

（3）杠铃推举时，杠铃下落到下颌处，对三角肌前束刺激得比较深。

（4）锁骨到下颌这个过程，三头肌参与发力的比重增大。

Attentions:

(1) Keep your shoulder joints steady and don't shake your body as long as you start to exercise.

(2) You should be careful not bend your body forward too much. Try to keep your torso upright when you do the barbell shoulder press.

(3) When the barbell is pushed, it falls to your chin and stimulates the anterior deltoid muscle more deeply.

(4) The process from clavicle to chin increases the proportion of triceps involved in exerting force.

图 4–2–20　杠铃颈前推举

Fig.4–2–20　Barbell shoulder press

21. 杠铃颈后推举 Barbell Press Behind Neck

锻炼部位：三角肌后束、背阔肌、大小圆肌、冈下肌、斜方肌，以及其他上背部肌肉。

Muscles exercised: Posterior deltoid, latissimus dorsi muscle, teres major, teres minor, infraspinatus muscle, trapezius muscle, and other upper back muscles.

动作要领：

（1）最好采用坐姿，紧靠座椅，两手持杠铃置于颈后肩上，上体保持挺胸收腹紧腰的姿势。

（2）随即吸气，持杠铃向上推起至头顶后上方两臂完全伸直为止，稍停 2～3 秒，再慢慢放下还原。

（3）注意放下负重时尽可能向下，然后开始重复。（图 4-2-21）

Behavioral essentials:

(1) It is better to start with a seated position, let your back close to the seat. Use both hands hold barbell, place it on the back of the neck and tighten your chest and waist.

(2) Then inhale, hold the barbell up to the top of the head and until the upper arms are fully extended. Stop for 2 to 3 seconds, and then slowly lower the barbell to the original place.

(3) Be careful to make the barbell downward when you drop the load, and then start to repeat the actions. (Fig.4-2-21)

负荷强度：6 组，每组 12 次，每组间歇 20 秒。

Intensity: 6 sets in all, each set for 12 times, then taking a 20-second break.

注意事项：

（1）将动作幅度做到最大。

（2）握距不要太窄，也不要太宽。

（3）不要用力向前移动臀部。

Attentions:

(1) Maximize your amplitude of movement.

(2) The holding span should not be too narrow or too wide.

(3) Don't push your hips forward.

图 4-2-21　杠铃颈后推举
Fig.4-2-21　Barbell press behind neck

22. 仰卧杠铃臂屈伸 Barbell Lying Triceps Extension

锻炼部位：肱三头肌、胸大肌、前锯肌和背阔肌。

Muscles exercised: Triceps muscle of arm, pectoralis major, serratus anterior and latissimus dorsi.

动作要领：

（1）身体平躺在长凳上，双手窄握曲柄杠铃，两臂伸直，保持与肩同宽的位置并且垂直于身体。

（2）动作开始时吸气，此时上臂不动，弯曲肘关节，使前臂缓慢向头部上方下落，到离额头两厘米的位置时，运用肱三头肌的力量将前臂挺直，同时呼气，手臂再次垂直于身体时，停顿一秒钟再次下落。重复练习。（图 4-2-22）

Behavioral essentials:

(1) Lie flatly on the bench, narrow grip the crank-barbell and keep your arms straight. Let your arms as wide as a shoulder's distance and make it perpendicular to your body.

(2) Inhale at the beginning of the movement. At this time, do not move the upper arm, bend the elbow joint and let the forearm slowly fall from the head. When it is two centimeters away from the forehead, use the force of the triceps to straighten the arm and exhale. When the arm is perpendicular to the body again, pause for a second and fall again. Then repeat the exercise. (Fig.4-2-22)

负荷强度：3 组，每组 12 次，每组间歇 15 秒。

Intensity: 3 sets in all, each set for 12 times, then taking a 15-second break.

注意事项：

（1）如果肘关节力量薄弱，可以不将手臂完全伸直，以避免受伤。

（2）大重量练习挺直手臂时，应尽量用意识克制使身体不离开平凳。

（3）接近力竭的时候，垂直的上臂可以稍稍向头的方向倾斜，借一点上胸的力量再做几次，可以让肱三头肌得到更多的刺激。

（4）双臂起落时双肘的距离保持不变，刺激肱三头肌中部位置。

Attentions:

(1) If the power of the elbows is weak, the arm needs not to be fully extended in order not to be injured.

(2) When exercising with a large weight and straightening your arms, try to restrain your body from leaving the flat stool.

(3) When you are close to exhaustion, the vertical upper arm can be tilted slightly in the direction of the head. By doing the exercise a few more times with the strength of the upper chest, you can let your triceps get more stimulation.

(4) Do not change the distance between the elbows when the arms are raised and lowered, and the middle part of the triceps is guaranteed to be stimulated.

图 4-2-22　仰卧杠铃臂屈伸

Fig.4-2-22　Barbell lying triceps extension

23. 窄握杠铃推举 Close Grip Barbell Press

锻炼部位：主要锻炼肱三头肌，对胸大肌的内侧、三角肌前束也有锻炼。

Muscles exercised: Triceps muscle of arm, inside of pectoralis major, and deltoid anterior.

动作要领：

（1）仰卧在长凳上，两脚平踏在地上，以维持身体平衡。两手握住横杠中间，窄握，间距为一掌宽。

（2）固定肘，横杠置于胸前，然后两上臂靠近体侧内夹，用肱三头肌收缩力量将两臂完全伸直，持杠铃支撑在两肩上方。

（3）两臂慢慢弯曲落下至横杠触及胸部，然后向上推起至开始位置，重复练习。（图 4-2-23）

Behavioral essentials:

(1) Lie on the bench with your feet on the floor to keep your body's balance. Close grip the middle of the horizontal bar at about one hand width.

(2) Fix your elbows, place the bar before the chest, and then place the upper arms close to the side of the body. Shrink the triceps to straighten the arms completely. Stretch the arms and hold the barbell above your shoulders.

(3) Slowly bend your arms until the bar touches your chest, then push them up to the starting position and repeat the exercise. (Fig.4-2-23)

负荷强度：3 组，每组 12 次，每组间歇 20 秒。

Intensity: 3 sets in all, each set for 12 times, then taking a 20-second break.

注意事项：

（1）注意宽握和窄握的区别：宽握卧推主要锻炼胸大肌，由内侧向外侧发展；窄握才是主要锻炼肱三头肌。

（2）控制好呼吸，用意识控制肱三头肌发力将杠铃推起。

Attentions:

(1) Pay attention to the difference between wide grip and narrow grip: wide grip bench press mainly exercise the pectoralis major muscle from the inside to the outside. Narrow grip mainly exercise the triceps.

(2) Control your breathing and try to use your triceps to push the barbell up.

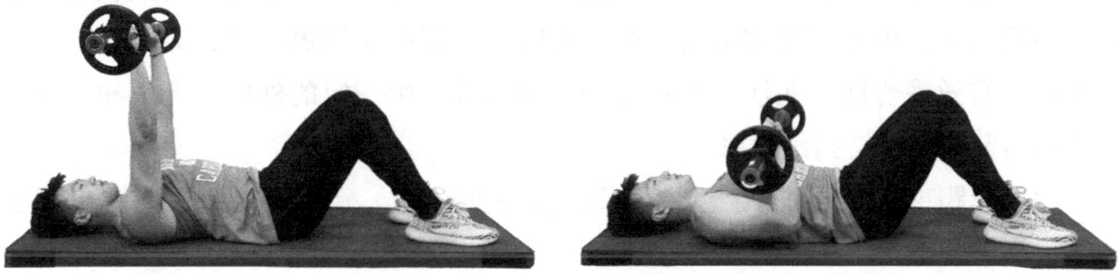

图 4-2-23　窄握杠铃推举

Fig.4-2-23　Close grip barbell press

24. 直立杠铃弯举 Standing Barbell Curl

锻炼部位：重点锻炼肱二头肌内侧头和腹肌。

Muscles exercised: Inside biceps brachii and abdominal muscles.

动作要领：

（1）身体直立，中握距（同肩宽）正握杠铃，垂于体前。

（2）两上臂贴紧身体两侧、向上弯举，注意力集中在整个肱二头肌上，至肱二头肌完全收紧稍停。

（3）缓慢控制地还原，以使肘部得到完全的伸展，如果屈臂则难以刺激到嵌入肘弯的肱二头肌下端。（图 4-2-24）

Behavioral essentials:

(1) Stand upright, holding the barbell in the medium part (shoulder width apart) and hanging it in front of your body.

(2) The upper arms are attached closely to both sides of your body, bend upward, pay attention to the entire biceps brachii to make the biceps brachii completely tightened.

(3) Then slowly return to the original condition so that the elbow can be fully stretchedyou' re your arms are bent ,it can be difficult to stimulate the lower end of the biceps muscle. (Fig.4-2-24)

负荷强度：3 组，每组 12 次，每组间歇 15 秒。

Intensity: 3 sets in all, each set for 12 times, then taking a 15-second break.

注意事项：

（1）整个运动过程中保持身体挺直，不要前后晃动。杠铃如果过重，你应当控制动作的幅度，否则容易分散肱二头肌受力，导致肌肉紧张度下降，增加下背部受伤的可能。

（2）直杠弯举与曲杠弯举区别：曲杠弯举角度符合手臂的内旋自然状态，前臂参与用力少，可保证更多负荷在肱二头肌上，刺激作用更明显，即旋后位可比旋前位更有效锻炼肱二头肌。直杠弯举迫使前臂产生一定的外旋，上举和下放时上臂和前臂都能保持持续紧张。

（3）握距变化：宽握距主要锻炼肱二头肌短头，窄握距主要锻炼肱二头肌长头。

（4）当杠铃举起时上抬肘部，可使肱二头肌得到更好的收缩，同时锻炼三角肌前部。

（5）为使这一动作更加精确可控，可以背靠墙壁，使肩胛骨紧贴在墙壁上。

Attentions:

(1) Keep your body upright during the exercise. Don't move back and forth. If

the barbell is too heavy, you should control the amplitude of the action. Because if the amplitude is too large, it tends to distract the strength on the biceps, leading to decreased muscle tension and increased risk of lower back injuries.

(2) Differences between barbell curl and Ez-bar curls: Ezor cambered bar's bending angle in accordance with the arm in natural state, less strength generated by forearm but more by the biceps, the stimulating effects can be more apparent, supinator position is more effective than pronator position to exercise the biceps. Ezor Ez-bar curls forces the forearm to rotate outwards to a certain degree. Both the upper and lower arms can maintain continuous tension.

(3) Change of grip width: Wide grip mainly exercises the short head of biceps brachium, and narrow grip mainly exercises the long head of biceps brachium.

(4) Lift the elbow when pushing up the barbell, the biceps brachii can get a better contraction and exercise the front of the deltoid muscle the same time.

(5) To make this more precise and controllable, you can lean against the wall with your back and your shoulder blades against the wall.

图 4–2–24　直立杠铃弯举

Fig. 4–2–24　Standing barbell curl

25. 杠铃俯身划船 Barbell Bent-over Row

锻炼部位：背阔肌。

Muscles exercised: Latissimus dorsi.

动作要领：

（1）膝关节稍稍弯曲，双脚分开稍稍超过臀部的宽度。上半身从臀部的位置向前倾斜，约与地面呈 30°　。采用手心朝下的方式握住杠铃杆，握距与肩同宽。手臂自然下垂，充分伸展背部肌肉。

（2）保持腹肌紧绷，用背部肌肉的力量把杠铃拉向下腹部。在动作的最高点，把两个肩胛骨靠拢，充分收紧背部肌肉。然后，保持对杠铃的控制，缓慢返回起始位置。（图 4-2-25）

Behavioral essentials:

(1) Knee joint bend slightly, feet apart and the width exceeds hip slightly. The upper body leans forward from the hips, at an angle of about 30 degrees to the ground.Hold the barbell bar with the palm downward and the grip is as wide as the shoulder.Arms naturally droop and stretch back muscles.

(2) Keep the abdominal muscle tight and use the strength of the back muscle to pull the barbell down to the abdomen. At the peaking of action, pull your shoulder blades together and tighten your back muscles. Then, keep control of the barbell and slowly return to the starting position. (Fig.4-2-25)

负荷强度：6 组，每组 12 次，每组间歇 20 秒。

Intensity: 6 sets in all, each set for 12 times, then taking a 20-second break.

注意事项：

（1）双手夹紧身体两侧。

（2）身体塌腰、挺胸、收紧腰腹部。

（3）拉起杠时呼气，回放杠铃时吸气。

Attentions:

(1) Keep your hands on both sides of your body.

(2) Arch the back, chest out and tighten your waist and abdomen.

(3) Exhale when pulling up the barbell and inhale when playing back the barbell.

图 4–2–25 杠铃俯身划船
Fig.4–2–25 Barbell bent–over row

26. “T”杠俯身划船 T-bar Bent-over Row

锻炼部位：背阔肌中部（内侧）、大圆肌。

Muscles exercised: Middle (medial) part of latissimus dorsi and teres major.

动作要领：

（1）两脚分开站立，两腿自然伸直，挺胸塌腰体前屈，两手臂伸直正握住“T”杠把柄。

（2）吸气，用背阔肌的收缩力量，使“T”杠提起至胸腹间，稍停 2～3 秒。

（3）呼气，持杠缓慢放下还原。（图 4-2-26）

Behavioral essentials:

(1) With your feet apart and legs straight, chest out and arch your back and bending forward while holding the handle of the T-bar.

(2) Inhale, using the contractile force of the latissimus dorsi muscle, lift the T-bar between the chest and abdomen, and pause for 2-3 seconds

(3) Exhale and slowly lower the bar to restore it. (Fig.4-2-26)

负荷强度：6 组，每组 12 次，每组间歇 20 秒。

Intensity: 6 sets in all, each set for 12 times, then taking a 20-second break.

注意事项：

（1）提拉“T”杠时两臂要贴近体侧，上体要始终保持挺胸，这样就有利于背阔肌的收缩。

（2）放下至两臂下垂时，两肩胛骨应放松，使背阔肌充分伸长，但“T”杠不能触地。

（3）动作过程中身体不要上下起伏。

（4）注意保护腰部，最好使用腰带。

Attentions:

(1) The arms should be close to the side of the body when pulling the T-bar, and the upper body should always be straight, which is conducive to the contraction of the latissimus dorsi muscle.

(2) When you drooped your arms, the scapula should be relaxed to fully extend the latissimus dorsi muscle, but the T-bar should not touch the ground.

图 4-2-26　“T”杠俯身划船
Fig.4-2-26　T-bar bent-over row

(3) Don’t let your body up

and down during the action.

(4) Be cautious to protect your waist, preferably with a waistband.

27. 负重耸肩 Weight-bearing Shrug

锻炼部位：肩侧斜方肌、颈肌和上背肌群。

Muscles exercised: Acromial trapezius, cervical muscle and upper back muscles.

动作要领：

（1）自然站立，两手背向前，持杠铃或哑铃，下垂在腿前。

（2）两肩同时向上耸起，使肩峰尽量触及耳朵，然后在这个顶点位置上慢慢地使两肩向后转，再慢慢地由后向下转至两臂下垂的原位。重复做。在耸肩过程中，不要屈肘。（图 4-2-27）

Behavioral essentials:

(1) Stand naturally with the opisthenar forward, hold a barbell or dumbbells and hanging it in front of your legs.

(2) Shrug your shoulders up at the same time, try to make your acromion touch the ears, turn back slowly when the acromion reach a fit high, then slowly turn your shoulders to the original position. Repeat this action. Don't bend your elbows while shrugging. (Fig.4-2-27)

负荷强度：3 组，每组 12 次，每组间歇 15 秒。

Intensity: 3 sets in all, each set for 12 times, then taking a 15-second break.

注意事项：

（1）严格地按照要求完成整个动作，即两肩尽量向两耳靠近，保持一会儿，不要屈肘。

（2）如果使手腕稍屈，并使两肘尖向外转，对肩侧斜方肌的收缩效果更有效。

（3）与其他身体部位一样，尽量使动作多样化。

Attentions:

(1) You can do the whole thing strictly as required, that is, keep your shoulders as close to your ears as possible, hold them for a while, and don't bend your elbows.

(2) If you bend your wrist slightly and turn the tip of your elbows outward, this is more effective for the contraction of the acromial trapezius muscle.

(3) Like other body parts, try to diversify your movements.

图 4–2–27　负重耸肩
Fig.4–2–27　Weight–bearing shrug

28. 负重躬身 Good-morning

锻炼部位：竖脊肌、臀大肌。

Muscles exercised: Erector spinae and gluteus maximus.

动作要领：

（1）两手持铃置于颈后肩上，挺胸、收腹、紧腰，两手必须托牢杠铃。

（2）吸气，上体向前慢慢弯下，至腰背部与地面平行为止，这时臀部应向后移，使身体重心处于脚跟后方，稍停 3～4 秒；

（3）呼气，以腰背肌肉的力量挺身起立还原，还原后再自然呼吸。重复此练习，动作过程中两腿膝盖微屈。（图 4-2-28）

Behavioral essentials:

(1) Hold the bell with your hands on the back of the neck and shoulders, straighten your chest, close your abdomen, tighten your waist, and hold the barbell firmly in both hands.

(2) Inhale and bend the upper body forward completely until the back of the waist is parallel to the ground. At this point, the hips should move backward, so that the body's center of gravity is behind the heel, and pause for 3-4 seconds.

(3) Exhale with the strength of the lumbar back muscle, stand upright and restore, and then breathe naturally. Repeat. The legs bend slightly at the knee during the action. (Fig.4-2-28)

负荷强度：3 组，每组 12 次，每组间歇 15 秒。

Intensity: 3 sets in all, each set for 12 times, then taking a 15-second break.

注意事项：

（1）初学者可以先不负重，当适应动作且腰部力量增加后，再适当负重。

（2）动作过程中，腰背部必须始终挺直；上体前屈时尽量慢些，切忌突然快速屈体，防止腰背部肌肉拉伤。

（3）动作过程中微屈膝盖，则重量负荷集中锻炼竖脊肌和臀大肌，动作过程中直腿，则重心落在大腿的股二头肌上，这就是二者的区别，也是锻炼的关键，可以在锻炼时仔细体会。

Attentions:

(1) For beginners, perform bending can free from load, as long as you adapted to the action and felt the power of your waist become stronger, then you can consider loading much.

(2) During the exercise, the waist and back must always be straight and upright. When make your upper body bend forward, try to slow down as much as possible. Avoid bending your body suddenly to prevent from pulling your dorsal muscle.

(3) Keep the knee slightly bend during the movement and focus on exercising the erector spinae and gluteus maximus. If you choose to unbend your legs, the focus then focus on the biceps femoris muscle in the thigh, this is the difference between bend and unbend your legs. And that is also the key point for the exercise, you can taste it during the exercise.

图 4-2-28　负重躬身

Fig.4-2-28　Good-morning

29. 屈腿硬拉 Stiff-legged Dead Lift

锻炼部位：竖脊肌，也能锻炼到臀大肌。

Muscles exercised: Erector spinae and gluteus maximus.

动作要领：

（1）双脚呈“V”字形站立，杠铃放体前，屈膝俯身，双手握杠铃。用力伸膝提铃，稍停。然后屈膝，缓慢下降还原。为提高锻炼效果，屈膝下降时杠铃不触及地面。

（2）拉到最高点时，双肩尽量外展，抬头挺胸，停滞 3 秒。还原，重复。

（图 4-2-29）

Behavioral essentials:

(1) Stand with your feet in a "V" shape. And put the barbell in front of you, bend your knees and body, and hold the barbell in both hands. Using hamstring muscles to extend the knee and lift the bell. Pause for a while. Then bend your knees and slowly return to the original position. To improve the effect of exercise, when drop the barbell, you must keep it above the ground slightly.

(2) Pull it to the highest point, extend your shoulders as far as you can, lift your head and keep your chest out for 3 seconds, return to the original condition and repeat. (Fig.4-2-29)

负荷强度：6 组，每组 8 次，每组间歇 25 秒。

Intensity: 6 sets in all, each set for 8 times, then taking a 25-second break.

注意事项：

（1）注意区别屈腿硬拉和直腿硬拉：屈腿硬拉是锻炼竖脊肌的最好办法，直腿硬拉则主要锻炼股二头肌。

（2）动作平稳，提拉杠铃时不能含胸弓腰，要抬头、腰背绷紧，上体始终保持紧张状态，否则容易损伤腰椎；提拉杠铃至极限时腰背不要后仰，意念要始终在后背部。

Attentions:

(1) Pay Attention to the differences between stiff-legged dead lift and dead lift: stiff-legged dead lift is the best way to exercise the erector spinac, dead lift is mainly for exercising femoral biceps in the thigh.

(2) Keep smooth and stable. When lifting the barbell, you must keep your body upright and rise your head, tighten your back and waist. Keep the upper part of your body always under pressure, or your vertebra lumbalis may be injured. Don't arch your lower back when you lift the barbell to the peak, your focus should always on your back.

图 4-2-29 屈腿硬拉
Fig.4-2-29 Stiff-legged dead lift

30. 史密斯卧推 Smith Press

锻炼部位：胸大肌。

Muscles exercised: Pectoralis major.

动作要领：

（1）在史密斯机上调整好长凳位置和角度：平板卧推时长凳处于水平位置，斜上推时长凳角度约 30°，斜下推时长凳角度约 20°；保持卧推上举时杠铃轴线落在胸部相应部位；采用比肩宽的握距，使胸大肌获得充分伸展和彻底收缩。

（2）当杠铃推起至两臂伸直时，必须使胸大肌处于"顶峰收缩"状态，稍停。

（3）上推时用鼻呼气，还原时用口吸气。（图 4-2-30）

Behavioral essentials:

(1) Adjust the position and angle of the Smith: The flat bench press is in a horizontal position, upward bench press about 30 degrees, and downward about 20 degrees. The barbell axis on the corresponding part of the chest when pushing up and lifting. The pectoralis major muscle is fully extended and contracted by using a wider grip than the shoulder.

(2) When the barbell is lifted until the arms are stretched straight, the pectoralis major must be kept in a state of "peak contraction" and stopped slightly.

(3) Exhale with your nose when pushing up, and inhale through your mouth when restoring. (Fig.4-2-30)

负荷强度：6 组，每组 8 次，每组间歇 25 秒。

Intensity: 6 sets in all, each set for 8 times, then taking a 25-second break.

注意事项：

（1）腰、臀不要抬离凳子，握距比肩宽。

（2）史密斯机适合初学者初步掌握卧推的技巧；对于中高级健身者，可以用来冲击极限大重量来提高卧推能力；先衰竭训练法中可用来辅助，于哑铃或杠铃卧推后紧接着进行史密斯卧推。

Attentions:

(1) Don't lift your hips and waist away from the bench. Hold them wider than your shoulders.

(2) The Smith machine is suitable for beginners to preliminarily master the skills of supine pushing. For middle and advanced fitness, it can be used to shock extreme heavy weight to improve the ability of supine pushing. The first failure

training method can be used to assist dumbbells or barbell supine pushing followed by Smith supine pushing.

图 4-2-30 史密斯卧推
Fig.4-2-30 Smith press

31. 平板杠铃卧推 Bench Barbell Press

锻炼部位：胸大肌。

Muscles exercised: Pectoralis major.

动作要领：

（1）采用宽握距，使胸大肌获得充分伸展和彻底收缩；要求躯干和胸部向上挺起成桥形，两肩下沉，横杠放在胸上置乳头上 1 厘米处；当杠铃推起至两臂伸直时，必须使胸大肌处于“顶峰收缩”状态，稍停。

（2）上推时用鼻呼气，还原时用口吸气。（图 4-2-31）

Behavioral essentials:

(1) Wide grip width is adopted to fully stretch and contract the pectoralis major muscle; The torso and chest should be raised in a shape of bridge, sink your shoulders, and the barbell should be placed on the chest at a height of 1 cm above the nipple. When the barbell is lifted until the arms are straight, the pectoralis major must be kept in a state of “peak contraction” and stopped for a while.

(2) Exhale with the nose when pushing up, and inhale with the mouth when restoring. (Fig.4-2-31)

负荷强度：6 组，每组 8 次，每组间歇 25 秒。

Intensity: 6 sets in all, each set for 8 times, then taking a 25-second break.

注意事项：

（1）腰、臀不要抬离卧推凳。

（2）双脚的位置：两腿分开呈 45°，平放在地上，以获得有力支撑。如果把脚踩到板凳上，稳定性会比较差，需要分担一部分力量控制核心肌群的稳定。当然，在史密斯机器上把脚放在凳子上就没有这一顾虑，其能有效阻止腰腹协助发力，更集中锻炼胸大肌。

（3）不同的握距刺激肌肉的重点也不同：比肩略窄锻炼中部胸大肌和肱三头肌；与肩同宽锻炼整个胸肌；比肩稍宽锻炼胸肌外侧；再宽侧重锻炼三角肌后束。

Attentions:

(1) Don't lift your hips and waist away from the bench press.

(2) Position of feet: The legs are separated into a 45-degree Angle and laid flat on the ground to provide strong support. If you put your foot on the bench, the stability will be poor. You need to share some of the strength to control the stability of the core muscle group. Of course, you can put your foot on the stool without this concern on Smith's machine, and it can effectively prevent the waist and abdomen from assisting the hair, and it can exercise the chest muscle in isolation.

(3) Different grip distances stimulate different muscle emphases: Exercise the midsection pectoralis major muscle and triceps slightly narrower than the shoulder; Exercise the entire chest muscle with shoulder width apart. Slightly wider than the shoulder exercises the lateral side of the pectoral muscle; The wider the back of the deltoid muscle is the focus.

图 4-2-31　平板杠铃卧推

Fig.4-2-31　Bench barbell press

32. 上斜杠铃卧推 Incline Barbell Press

锻炼部位：胸大肌的上部及外侧翼上端。

Muscles exercised: Upper part and peripheral top of musculi pectoralis major.

动作要领：

仰卧在可调节斜度的长凳上，头部处于高位，使躯干与地面呈 30° ～40°，杠铃应垂直向上推起至处于肩关节的垂直线上，使胸大肌处于“顶峰收缩”位，稍停。(图 4-2-32)

Behavioral essentials :

Lie on your back on a bench in the adjustable angle, rise your head high, the angle between the torso and the ground is 30-40 degrees, the barbell should be lifted vertically the shoulder joint on the vertical line, keep your pectoralis major under a state of “peak contraction” , then stop for a while. (Fig.4-2-32)

负荷强度：6 组，每组 8 次，每组间歇 25 秒。

Intensity: 6 sets in all, each set for 8 times, then taking a 25-second break.

注意事项：

斜板角度的变化对胸部的练习效果有所影响。如横杠贴近乳头部位上推，对胸大肌内侧及外侧训练效果为佳。如横杠贴近颈部，对胸大肌上半部和里面半部训练效果最佳。

Attentions:

The change of Angle of inc-lined plate also changed the effect of chest practice.If the horizontal bar is pushed up close to the nipple, the training effect on the inside and outside of the pectoralis major muscle is better. If the horizontal bar is close to the neck, and it has the best effect on the upper part of the pectoralis major muscle and the inner part.

图 4–2–32　上斜杠铃卧推

Fig.4–2–32　Incline barbell press

33. 颈后深蹲 Back Squat

锻炼部位：股四头肌、所有收肌、臀肌及全部竖脊肌。

Muscles exercised: Quadriceps, all adductors, gluteus and all erector spinae.

动作要领：

两腿分开，双手持杠铃置于颈后，做蹲起动作。此动作可以采用窄、中、宽步距进行多方式的锻炼以全方位地刺激肌肉。（图 4-2-33）

Behavioral essentials:

Stand with your legs apart and hold the barbells on your back shoulder, perform squats. This action can be used to narrow, medium and wide steps for a variety of exercises to achieve a full range of muscle stimulation. (Fig.4-2-33)

负荷强度：6 组，每组 8 次，每组间歇 25 秒。

Intensity: 6 sets in all, each set for 8 times, then taking a 25-second break.

注意事项：

（1）从深蹲练习时的安全角度来讲，颈前深蹲较颈后深蹲危险。如果负重相同的重量，颈前深蹲需要更强的腿部控制力，这就需要练习者有一定的健身基础；颈后深蹲则可以借助手臂、臀部等的力量。因此，一般颈前深蹲的负重重量小于颈后深蹲的负重重量。

（2）从练习者将杠铃拿起和放下的角度来讲，颈前深蹲相对颈后深蹲比较简单和安全。因为颈前深蹲时杠铃不需要举过头顶放到颈后或者从颈后放到颈前，只需要放到与肩同高的位置。

Attentions:

(1) From the perspective of safety in the practice of full squat, front squat is more dangerous than the back squat. If the front squat and back squat front bear the same weight, the former needs more power generated by the legs, which requires the practitioner should possess certain fitness base. The back squat can borrow the power through arms and hips and etc. Therefore, the weight of front squat is less than back squat in average.

图 4–2–33　颈后深蹲
Fig.4–2–33　Back squat

(2) From the perspective of lifting and putting down the barbell, the front squat is relatively simple and safe than back squat. Because it does not need to lift barbell over the head, then put it on the back of your neck, or from the back of the neck to the front of the neck, just need to place it in the same height with the shoulder.

34. 仰卧提臀 Hip Thrus

锻炼部位：臀大肌。

Muscles exercised: Gluteus maximus.

动作要领：

（1）仰卧，使上背靠着箱子或者长凳，屈膝，双脚着地，腹部可以杠铃作为负重。

（2）呼气，保持腹肌处于收缩状态，收缩臀大肌，并向上挺起臀部，尽可能抬到最高，停留 1～2 秒；吸气，慢慢恢复到原位，重复。（图 4-2-34）

Behavioral essentials:

(1) Lie on your back with your upper back against a box or bench, bend your knees, and land on your feet. The abdomen can bear the weight of the barbell.

(2) Exhale, keeping your abs in a contraction state, contracting the gluteus maximus muscle, and raising your hips as high as possible, for 1-2 seconds.Inhale, slowly return to position, repeat. (Fig.4-2-34)

负荷强度：6 组，每组 8 次，每组间歇 25 秒。

Intensity: 6 sets in all, each set for 8 times, then taking a 25-second break.

注意事项：

（1）臀部发力，手臂和上背部不要下压借力。

（2）躯干上抬时以臀部为着力点和上移的中心，而不是中下背部。

（3）肩和上背部同时作为支点提供稳固支撑，不要将上背部抬起，否则很容易损伤肩部和颈椎。

Attentions:

(1) The power should be generated by the hips, arm and upper back do not press down to borrow power.

(2) When the torso is lifted, the hips are the main points of the strength and the center for the upward movement instead of middle and lower back.

(3) Both the shoulder and upper back should act as the same fulcrum to provide firm support, and do not try to lift the upper back, which can easily make the shoulders

and neck injured.

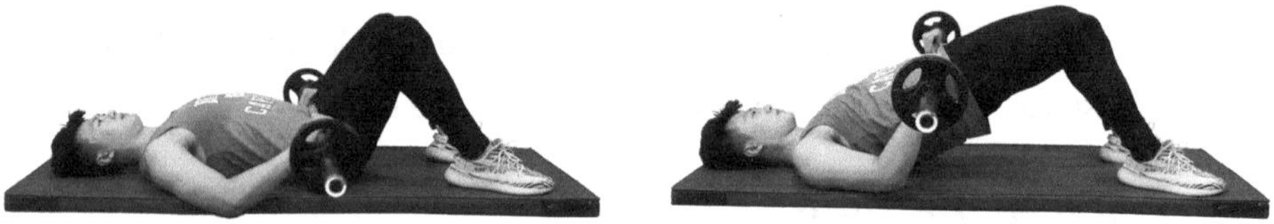

图 4-2-34 仰卧提臀
Fig.4-2-34 Hip thrus

35. 史密斯深蹲 Smith-machine Squat

锻炼部位：股四头肌、臀大肌。

Muscles exercised: Quadriceps and Gluteus maximus.

动作要领：

深蹲时动作路径是唯一的，一般采用与颈后杠铃深蹲类似的深蹲，技术因素功效比较接近，不再详述。（图 4-2-35）

Behavioral essentials:

The action path of deep squat is unique, generally use the barbell squat behind the neck similar to deep squat, technical factors of similar efficacy, no longer detailed. (Fig.4-2-35)

负荷强度：6 组，每组 8 次，每组间歇 25 秒。

Intensity: 6 sets in all, each set for 8 times, then taking a 25-second break.

注意事项：

（1）双脚与杠铃在同一垂直面，或者身体重心更靠后时，主要锻炼股四头肌，而对股二头肌、臀大肌的刺激程度降低到最小；随着并拢的双脚向前移动，锻炼刺激逐渐向股二头肌和臀大肌转移。

（2）虽然自由负重深蹲常被认为是增大腿部肌肉块的最佳动作，但如果在常规训练中配合史密斯机深蹲和腿举，效果会更好。

Attentions:

(1) When both feet and barbells are in the same vertical plane, or when the body's center of gravity is further back, the quadriceps are mainly exercised, while the stimulation to the biceps and gluteus maximus muscles is minimized. As the closed feet move forward, the exercise stimulus is gradually transferred to the biceps femoris and gluteus maximus.

(2) While free weight squat is often considered the best way to increase muscle mass in the legs, it is better to combine Smith machine squats and leg lifts in regular training.

图 4-2-35 史密斯深蹲
Fig.4-2-35 Smith-machine squat

36. 箭步蹲杠铃 Barbell Lunges

锻炼部位：以股四头肌为主，对臀大肌、股二头肌及小腿肌群也有锻炼效果。

Muscles exercised: Mainly for quadriceps, and also has exercise effect on gluteus maximus, femoral biceps and calf muscles.

动作要领：

（1）双手持一杠铃自然直臂垂于体侧或肩负杠铃，双手持杠铃屈肘置于肩上，两脚开立与髋同宽，目视前方，挺胸收腹。

（2）一脚向前迈出一步，下蹲使膝关节与踝关节在同一垂线上，另一腿向后伸直，重量均匀分布在两腿上。沉髋、后腿屈膝下蹲至膝关节接近地面，稍顿，循原路还原。（图 4-2-36）

Behavioral essentials:

(1) Hold a barbells in both hands, with straight arms hanging at the sides of the body or carrying barbells. Hold the barbells with elbows on the shoulders with both hands, stand with your feet shoulder-widt hapart, look straight ahead, keep your chest up and tuck in your stomach.

(2) One foot takes a step forward and the squat makes the knee and ankle joint in the same vertical line. The other leg extends backward and the weight is evenly distributed on both legs. Sink hip, hind leg kneels down to knee joint is close to the ground, follow the original path slightly. (Fig.4-2-36)

负荷强度：3 组，每组 12 次，每组间歇 15 秒。

Intensity: 3 sets in all, each set for 12 times, then taking a 15-second break.

注意事项：

（1）上身要始终保持正直，让重心垂直向下。身体不能后仰或前倾。垂直下蹲时，前腿小腿垂直地面，膝盖不要超过脚尖。

（2）箭步蹲的作用还体现在用于维持此动作身体平衡的肌肉的锻炼上。因此，初始时身体的不平衡属于锻炼的切入点，应加以关注。

（3）跨距太小会导致重心不稳，使腿部动作受限而得不到锻炼。跨距大时，下蹲过程中后腿应尽量保持绷直；跨距小时，前腿的膝盖可向前冲出。

（4）箭步蹲动作过程中，双腿不同的跨距锻炼的肌肉侧重有所区别，跨距越大越偏重于同时锻炼股四头肌、股二头肌和臀大肌，跨距越小越集中锻炼股四头肌。

Attentions:

(1) Always keep your upper body upright, and keep the main part of your body vertically downward. The body should not lean back or forwards. When squatting vertically, the shank of the front leg is vertical to the ground and the knee should not exceed the toe.

(2) The function of the lunge squat is also reflected on the muscle exercise which maintain the balance of the body when doing this action. Therefore, the unbalanced state should be improved, which is the entry point at the primary stage.

(3) The span should not be too small to make the main part of your body unstable and it may limit leg movements; When the span is large, the hind legs should be as straight as possible during the squat. The knee of the front leg can rush forward when the span is small.

图 4-2-36　箭步蹲杠铃
Fig.4-2-36　Barbell Lunges

(4) In performing squat movement, different spans have different effects of different body parts. A bigger span is biased on the biceps femoris and quadriceps, and glutes exercise at the same time. Smaller the span is, more exercise the quadriceps muscle gets.

37. 直腿硬拉 Stiff-legged Deadlift

锻炼部位：臀大肌、股二头肌。

Muscles exercised: Gluteus maximus, biceps femoris.

动作要领：

（1）两脚开立稍窄于肩；向前屈体，不要屈膝。两手正握杠铃，握距同肩宽，垂于体前，也可双手握一对哑铃，勿低头。

（2）直膝向前屈体至上体与地面平行，然后下背部肌肉收缩用力，脊柱前挺，上拉杠铃成开始姿势。提铃和还原过程腰要绷紧，不得含胸弓腰。（图 4-2-37）

Behavioral essentials:

(1) Stand with your feet apart, slightly narrower than the shoulder; Bend forward, don' t bend your knees. Hold barbell with your hands, hold distance with shoulder width to hang in front of the body, also can hold a pair of dumbbells, do not bow.

(2) Bends forward with straight knees to make upper body parallel to the ground, then the muscles of the lower back contract and exert themselves. The spine is straight forward, and the barbell is pulled up to the starting position. (Fig.4-2-37)

负荷强度：6 组，每组 8 次，每组间歇 25 秒。

Intensity: 6 sets in all, each set for 8 times, then taking a 25-second break.

注意事项：

（1）两腿始终直立，膝部勿弯曲。

（2）为使股二头肌得到充分刺激，采用与髋同宽的平行站立。为提高难度和强度，可采用垫木直腿硬拉，下放杠铃时不要触及地面，目的是让股二头肌和腰背部保持张紧力，让受力集中在目标肌上。

（3）要控制住重量，动作平稳，提铃和还原过程中腰要绷紧，不得含胸弓腰。

Attentions:

(1) Keep your legs upright and keep your knees straight.

(2) In order to fully stimulate the biceps femoris, stand parallel to the hip width. In order to improve the difficulty and strength, the padded straight leg can be pulled hard, and the barbell should not touch the ground when lowered. The purpose is to keep the biceps femoris muscle and the back of the waist tight, so that the force is concentrated on the target muscle.

(3) The weight should be controlled, and the movement should be stable. The waist should be tightened during bell lifting and reduction, and the waist should not contain

the chest arch.

图 4–2–37　直腿硬拉

Fig.4–2–37　Stiff–legged deadlift

第三节　瑞士球训练

Section 3　Swiss Ball Training

1. 双腿支撑俯卧撑 Push Up with Legs Supporting

锻炼部位：胸大肌、前锯肌、肱三头肌、腹直肌。

Muscles exercised: Pectoralis major, serratus anterior, triceps, rectus abdominis.

动作要领：

（1）将小腿和双脚搭在瑞士球球面上，双臂支撑于地面，身体保持成一条水平线。

（2）屈肘俯卧，脸尽量贴近地面。当上臂与地面平行时伸肘还原。（图 4-3-1）

Behavioral essentials:

(1) Place your lower legs and feet on the Swiss ball,use your arms to support your body on the ground. Keep your body horizontal.

(2) Do push ups and try to keep your face as close to the ground as possible. Unbend the extension elbow when the arm is parallel to the ground. (Fig.4-3-1)

负荷强度：3 组，每组 12 次，每组间歇 60 秒。

Intensity: 3 sets in all, each set for 12 times, then taking a 60-second break.

注意事项：

（1）训练初期双脚可以有一定间距，降低难度。后期可以逐渐缩小双脚间距，直到膝盖和脚踝并拢。

（2）完成动作时核心部位要保持紧张，身体始终要挺直，下降时小腿不能弯曲。

Attentions:

(1) At the beginning of training, the feet can be spaced apart to reduce difficulty. Later you can gradually narrow the space between your feet until your knees and ankles are together.

(2) The core should be kept tense, the body should always be upright, and the lower leg should not be bent.

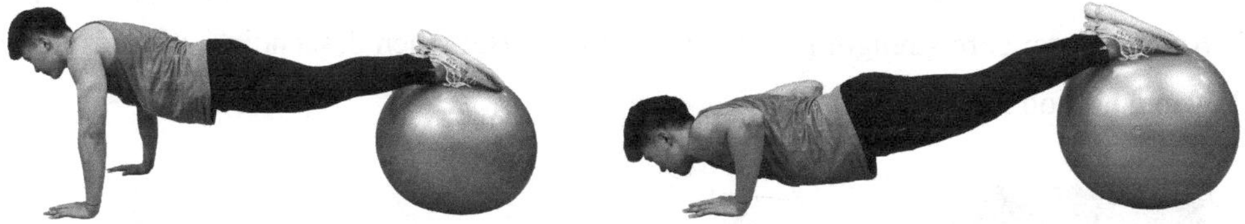

图 4–3–1　双腿支撑俯卧撑

Fig.4–3–1　Push up with legs supporting

2. 双脚脚尖支撑俯卧撑 Push-up Supported on Both Toes

锻炼部位：胸大肌、前锯肌、肱三头肌、腹直肌。

Muscles exercised: Pectoralis major, serratus anterior, triceps, rectus abdominis.

动作要领：

（1）将小腿和双脚搭在瑞士球上，双臂支撑于地面。随后双手向前爬行，直到双脚脚尖支撑在瑞士球球面。

（2）屈肘俯卧，当上臂与地面平行时伸肘还原。（图 4-3-2）

Behavioral essentials:

(1) Put your legs and feet on the Swiss ball and use your arm support your body on the ground. Then crawl forward with both hands until your toes support the Swiss Ball.

(2) Do push ups. Unbend the bent elbow when the arm is parallel to the ground. (Fig.4-3-2)

负荷强度：3 组，每组 12 次，每组间歇 90 秒。

Intensity: 3 sets in all, each set for 12 times, then taking a 90-second break.

注意事项：

（1）双手向前爬行时，要等到双脚脚尖搭于球上，下肢完全由脚趾支撑时才能停止。

（2）完成动作时身体要保持挺直，保持脚尖立于球面，臀部不能塌陷。

（3）动作难度高于双腿支撑俯卧撑，因此需要更大的核心力量支撑。下降时身体要缓慢，不能过快。

Attentions:

(1) When crawling forward with both hands, stop when the toes are on the ball and the lower limbs are fully supported by the toes.

(2) Keep your body straight and keep your toes on the ball, your hips should not collapse.

(3) The difficulty of the movement is higher than that of leg support push ups, therefore greater core strength is needed to support. But when descending, it needs to be slow and not too fast.

图 4-3-2　双脚脚尖支撑俯卧撑
Fig.4-3-2　Push-up supported on both toes

3. 单腿支撑俯卧撑 Single Leg Supported Push-up Supported on One leg

锻炼部位：胸大肌、前锯肌、肱三头肌、腹直肌。

Muscles exercised: Pectoralis major, serratus anterior, triceps, rectus abdominis.

动作要领：

（1）将小腿和双脚搭在瑞士球球面上，双臂支撑于地面，身体保持成一条水平线。

（2）抬起一条腿，同时双臂屈肘俯卧。当上臂与地面平行时伸肘还原，抬起的腿不要落下。（图 4-3-3）

Behavioral essentials:

(1) Place your lower legs and feet on the Swiss ball,use your arms to supports to your body on the ground. Keep your body horizontal.

(2) Lift one leg and do push ups. When your upper arms are parallel to the ground, extend the elbows back and keep your higher leg over the Swiss ball. (Fig.4-3-3)

负荷强度：3 组，每一侧腿完成 12 次，完成两侧腿为一组，每组间歇 120 秒。

Intensity: 3 sets in all, each set for 12 times, complete both sides as one set, then taking a 120-second break.

注意事项：

（1）俯卧和撑起时注意身体挺直，躯干不能弯曲。

（2）完成动作时抬起的腿不能落下，保证只有一侧腿在支撑。

Attentions:

(1) When lowering and puching up, keep your body upright and avoid bending your torso.

(2) Keep your higher leg over the Swiss ball, and use only one leg to support your body.

图 4–3–3　单腿支撑俯卧撑

Fig.4–3–3　Single leg supported push–up supported on one leg

4. 双腿支撑爬行 Crawl with Legs Supporting

锻炼部位：三角肌、腹直肌、胸大肌。

Muscles exercised: Deltoid, rectus abdominis, pectoralis major.

动作要领：

（1）上体俯卧在瑞士球上。

（2）双手支撑地面，缓慢向前爬行。当双脚移动到瑞士球顶部时再向后爬行，还原到初始位置。（图 4-3-4）

Behavioral essentials:

(1) Lie on your stomach on the Swiss ball.

(2) Use your arms support your body on the ground. Then crawl forward slowly. When you move your feet to the top of the Swiss ball, crawl backwards and return to the original position. (Fig.4-3-4)

负荷强度：3 组，每组 8 次，每组间歇 60 秒。

Intensity: 3 sets in all, each set for 8 times, then taking a 60-second break.

注意事项：

（1）爬行时躯干挺直，身体要保持在一条直线上。

（2）缓慢移动，体验肌肉的用力，不要求速度。

Attentions:

(1) Keep your torso straight and your body in a straight line.

(2) Slowly move and experience muscle exertion without requiring speed.

图 4–3–4　双腿支撑爬行

Fig.4–3–4　Crawl with legs supporting

5. 单腿支撑爬行 Crawl with Single Leg Supporting

锻炼部位：三角肌、腹直肌、胸大肌。

Muscles exercised: Deltoid, rectus abdominis, pectoralis major.

动作要领：

（1）上体俯卧在瑞士球上。

（2）抬起一条腿，双手撑地缓慢向前爬行。当脚面移动到瑞士球顶部时向后返回。（图 4-3-5）

Behavioral essentials:

(1) Lie prostrate on the Swiss ball.

(2) Lift up one leg and crawl slowly forward with both hands supporting. Return backward when your feet reach the top of the Swiss ball. (Fig.4-3-5)

负荷强度：3 组，每组 8 次，每组间歇 60 秒。

Intensity: 3 sets in all, each set for 8 times, then taking a 60-second break.

注意事项：

（1）爬行过程中要保持臀部的水平，不能转动。肩部和臀部不能塌陷。

（2）抬起的腿要保持稳定，不能降低高度和摆动。

Attentions:

(1) Keep your buttock horizontal during crawling, and do not rotate. The shoulders and hips cannot collapse.

(2) The lifted leg should remain stable and not lower in height or swing.

图 4–3–5 单腿支撑爬行
Fig.4–3–5 Crawl with single leg supporting

6. 双球支撑俯卧撑 Push Ups on Two Balls

锻炼部位：胸大肌、前锯肌、肱三头肌、腹直肌。

Muscles exercised: Pectoralis major, serratus anterior, triceps, rectus abdominis.

动作要领：

（1）并排放置两个瑞士球，两臂支撑于瑞士球上，呈俯卧撑准备姿势。

（2）屈肘俯卧，俯卧至头部与支撑手平齐的位置时伸肘还原。（图 4-3-6）

Behavioral essentials:

(1) Place two Swiss balls side by side.Use your arms to support your body on the Swiss balls in a push-up position.

(2) Bend the elbows until the head and the supporting hand. (Fig.4-3-6)

负荷强度：3 组，每组 12 次，每组间歇 90 秒。

Intensity: 3 sets in all, each set for 12 times, then taking a 90-second break.

注意事项：

（1）保持身体挺直，臀部不能塌陷或翘起。

（2）前期练习时可以减少俯卧深度来增加适应性，后期则应在头与支撑手平齐后起身。

Attentions:

(1) Keep your body straight and your buttock should not collapse or rise.

(2) In the early stage, the prone depth can be reduced to increase the adaptability; In the later stage, the head should be in a horizontal plane with the supporting hand before getting up.

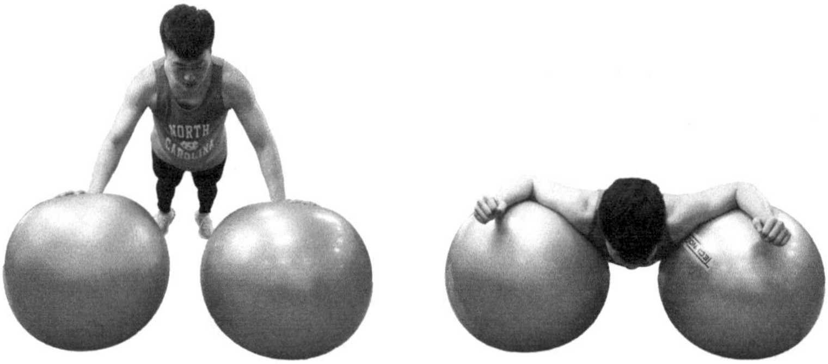

图 4–3–6　双球支撑俯卧撑
Fig.4–3–6　Push ups on two balls

7. 双肘支撑外扩内收 Elbows External Expansion and Adduction on Two Swiss Balls

锻炼部位：胸大肌、三角肌、肩胛下肌、大圆肌、斜方肌。

Muscles exercised: Pectoralis major, deltoid, subscapular muscle, teres major, trapezius.

动作要领：

（1）并排放置两个瑞士球，以两前臂支撑俯卧在瑞士球上。

（2）上臂外扩，推动瑞士球向两边移动。

（3）当上臂打开最大后，内收回位。（图 4-3-7）

Behavioral essentials:

(1) Place two Swiss balls side by side and lie prone on the Swiss balls with two forearms supporting on them.

(2) The upper arms expand to push the Swiss balls apart.

(3) When the upper arms move to the maximum extent, adduct to the starting position. (Fig.4-3-7)

负荷强度：3 组，每组 12 次，每组间歇 60 秒。

Intensity: 3 sets in all, each set for 12 times, then taking a 60-second break.

注意事项：

（1）身体挺直，当上臂打开与身体呈水平状态时才可以内收。

（2）上臂外扩时动作要缓慢，充分感受肌肉用力。

Attentions:

(1) Keep your body straight, and don't retract until your upper arms are open to the same horizontal plane with your body.

(2) When expanding your upper arms, move slowly to fully feel the muscle engagenment.

图 4-3-7　双肘支撑外扩内收

Fig.4-3-7　Elbows external expansion and adduction on two swiss balls

8. 前后滚动双球 Roll Double Balls

锻炼部位： 胸大肌、三角肌、腹直肌。

Muscles exercised: Pectoralis major, Deltoid, Rectus abdominis.

动作要领：

（1）并排放置两个瑞士球，双膝跪地，双手扶在瑞士球上部。

（2）双膝离地，支撑点变为双手和脚尖，慢慢向前滚球。

（3）身体前倾，将球面支撑点从双手过渡到前臂，滚球前进。

（4）向前滚动到身体尽量能控制的角度，维持姿势 3 秒后向后滚球还原。（图 4-3-8）

Behavioral essentials:

(1) Place two Swiss balls side by side, keep knees on the ground and hands on the top of the Swiss balls.

(2) Roll the ball forward slowly with both knees off the ground. Use hands and toes to support your body.

(3) Lean forwards, move the handholds on two balls from hands to forearms, and roll the balls forwards.

(4) Roll forwards as far as possible. Maintain the posture for 3 seconds, then roll back to the starting position. (Fig.4-3-8)

负荷强度： 8 组，每组 1 次，每组间歇 30 秒。

Intensity: 8 sets in all, each set for 1 times, then taking a 30-second break.

注意事项：

（1）脚尖支撑位置不变，不能移动下肢。

（2）臀部不能塌陷或翘起，上体要挺直。

（3）前进后退过程要缓慢，充分感受肌肉用力。

Attentions:

(1) Do not move your toes and lower legs.

(2) Do not collapse or raise your buttock and always keep your upper body straight.

(3) The process of moving forwards and backwards should be slow, and fully feel the muscle exertion.

图 4–3–8　前后滚动双球

Fig.4–3–8　Roll double balls

9. 双腿搭球卷腹 Crawl with Legs on a Swiss Ball

锻炼部位：腹直肌、髂腰肌。

Muscles exercised: Rectus abdominis, iliopsoas.

动作要领：

（1）上体平躺仰卧，双手抱于胸前或伸直向上，小腿搭于瑞士球球面，小腿与大腿夹住瑞士球。

（2）进行卷腹动作，上体向上抬起。在抬至最高点稍事停留后下降还原。（图 4-3-9）

Behavioral essentials:

(1) Lie flat on your back with your hands in front of your chest or straight up, and your shanks straight up on the Swiss ball.Clamp the Swiss ball between your shanks and thighs.

(2) Do an abdominal crunch to lift the upper body up. Stop for a while at the top and then restore slightly. (Fig.4-3-9)

负荷强度：6 组，每组 12 次，每组间歇 90 秒。

Intensity: 6 sets in all, each set for 12 times, then taking a 90-second break.

注意事项：

（1）卷腹时胸部尽量靠近大腿，在顶端稍作停留。

（2）下降时要缓慢，下一次动作不能依靠上一次的惯性。

Attentions:

(1) When you do abdominal crunch, move your chest close to your thighs as close as possible and stay there for a while.

(2) Move slowly when you lie down, do not the inertia.

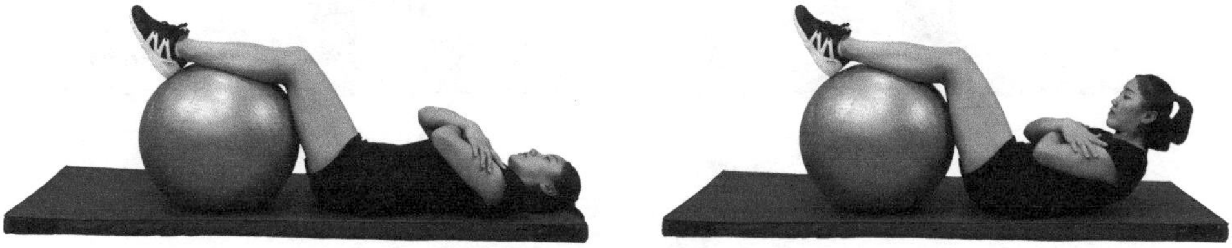

图 4-3-9 双腿搭球卷腹

Fig.4-3-9 Crawl with legs on a Swiss ball

10. 仰卧屈膝夹球转髋 Turn Your Hip with Bend Knees Clamping the Swiss Ball in Supine Posture

锻炼部位：腹内斜肌、腹外斜肌。

Muscles exercised: Internal oblique, external oblique.

动作要领：

（1）身体平躺于地面，双臂打开伸直。大腿与小腿呈 90° 弯曲夹住瑞士球两端侧上方。

（2）向身体一侧转髋，当身体感觉达到最大限度后转向另一侧。（图 4-3-10）

Behavioral essentials:

(1) Lie flat on the ground with arms open and straight. The upper side of the Swiss ball is gripped by a 90-degree bend between the your thighs and shanks.

(2) Turn your hip to one side of your body. Turn it as much as possible you can and then change the side. (Fig.4-3-10)

负荷强度：6 组，每组 12 次，每组间歇 60 秒。

Intensity: 6 sets in all, each set for 12 times, then taking a 60-second break.

注意事项：

（1）完成动作时背部和肩部要紧贴地面，不能离开。

（2）完成动作时核心要收紧，上体不能晃动。

Attentions:

(1) Keep your back and shoulders on the ground all the time, can' t go away.

(2) The core should be tightened and the upper body should not shake.

图 4–3–10 仰卧屈膝夹球转髋

Fig.4–3–10 Turn your hip with bend knees clamping the swiss ball in supine posture

11. 仰卧双腿夹球上摆 Life Your Legs with Bend Knees Clamping the Swiss Ball in Supine Posture

锻炼部位：腹直肌、髂腰肌。

Muscles exercised: Rectus abdominis, iliopsoas.

动作要领：

（1）平躺在地面，双手放在身体两侧。两小腿平放在瑞士球球面上，小腿和大腿呈 90° 夹住瑞士球。

（2）小腿和大腿夹球抬起，大腿最大限度贴近上体后放下。（图 4-3-11）

Behavioral essentials:

(1) Lie flat on the ground with your hands on the either side of the body. Place both legs on the Swiss ball, and clamp the ball with shanks and thighs.

(2) Use your shanks and thighs clamp the ball.Then lift it up to the maximum extent. Move it close to the upper body as much as you can. After that, put it down. (Fig.4-3-11)

负荷强度：6 组，每组 12 次，每组间歇 60 秒。

Intensity: 6 sets in all, each set for 12 times, then taking a 60-second break.

注意事项：

（1）完成动作时背部和肩部要紧贴地面。

（2）放球时要缓慢，下一次动作不能依靠上一次的惯性。

（3）小腿和大腿不能用力。

Attentions:

(1) Keep your back and shoulders on the ground all the time.

(2) Move slowly when you put down the ball, the next move can't rely on the last inertia.

(3) Don't use the power from your shanks and thighs.

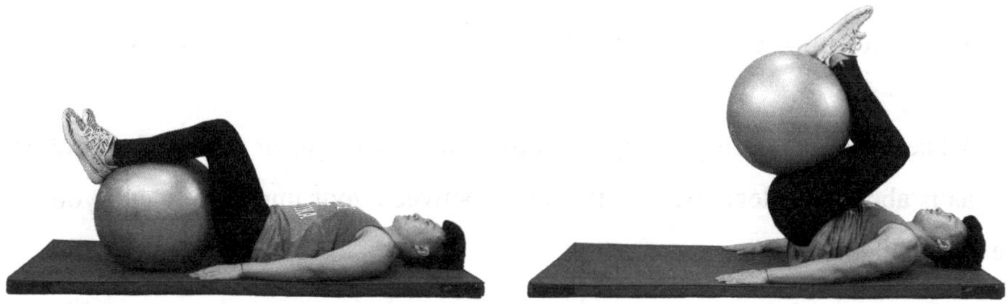

图 4–3–11　仰卧双腿夹球上摆

Fig.4–3–11　Life your legs with bend knees clamping the swiss ball in supine posture

12. 坐立仰卧起坐 Siting sit-ups

锻炼部位：腹直肌、髂腰肌、臀大肌。

Muscles exercised: Rectus abdominis, iliopsoas, gluteus maximus.

动作要领：

（1）端坐在平衡球上，小腿与大腿形成 90° 夹角。

（2）将双手放在头两侧，双脚向前迈出，臀部向瑞士球前方移动。

（3）移动过程中双腿自然分开与肩同宽，上体继续向后仰。当球面滚动到背部时还原。（图 4-3-12）

Behavioral essentials:

(1) Sit upright on the balance ball, keep your shanks form a 90-degree Angle to your thighs.

(2) Put your hands on both sides of your head, step forward and move your hip in

front of the Swiss ball.

(3) During the movement, legs naturally parted at shoulder width and lean back your upper body. Restores when the ball rolls to the back. (Fig.4-3-12)

负荷强度： 6 组，每组 12 次，每组间歇 60 秒。

Intensity: 6 sets in all, each set for 12 times, then taking a 60-second break.

注意事项：

（1）在双脚向前迈出开始动作后，以双脚为支点固定。在进行动作时不能移动，动作完成靠核心和腹直肌发力。

（2）仰卧起坐起止位置时上身与大腿的夹角约为 135°，结束时上身与大腿的夹角约为 90°。

Attentions:

(1) After your feet move forwards to start the movement, use your feet to support. Don't move during the movement.The action is performed by the core and rectus abdominis.

(2) The angle between your upper body and your thighs at the starting and ending positions is about 135 degrees. And the angle between your upper body and your thighs at the end is about 90 degrees.

图 4-3-12　坐立仰卧起坐

Fig.4-3-12　Siting sit-ups

13. 抱头体侧屈 Side Flexion with Hands on Head

锻炼部位： 腹外斜肌、腹内斜肌、竖脊肌、臀大肌。

Muscles exercised: External oblique, internal oblique, erector spinae, gluteus maximus.

动作要领：

（1）坐立在瑞士球上，随后双腿向前迈出，双手抱头，向一侧 90° 转动身体，髋关节支撑在瑞士球球面上。

（2）做单侧体侧屈动作，上体与地面几乎垂直时还原。（图 4-3-13）

Behavioral essentials:

(1) Sit on the Swiss ball, then leg forward with hands on your head, turn your body 90 degrees to one side.The hip is supported on the Swiss ball.

(2) Do one side bending and restore when your upper body is almost vertical to the ground. (Fig.4-3-13)

负荷强度：6 组，每侧动作每组 12 次，完成两侧为一组，每组间歇 90 秒。

Intensity: 6 sets in all, each set for 12 times, complete both sides as one set, then taking a 90-second break.

注意事项：

（1）动作开始时两脚分开约一步距离，练习时两腿可以轮换位置。

（2）作为支点的腿在进行动作时要保持稳定，不能发力帮助完成动作。

Attentions:

(1) Start with your feet about a step apart, your legs can rotate during practice.

(2) The leg as the fulcrum should be stable during the action. Don't use the power from this leg to help you finish the movement.

图 4-3-13　抱头体侧屈

Fig.4-3-13　Side flexion with hands on head

14. 瑞士球屈腿内收 Bend Your Legs on the Swiss Ball

锻炼部位：腹直肌、髂腰肌。

Muscles exercised: Rectus abdominis, iliopsoas.

动作要领：

（1）双腿搭在瑞士球球面上，两臂与肩同宽支撑地面。

（2）保持上半身姿势不变，双腿向前弯曲，使瑞士球在脚踝下向前滚动，直至腹肌收缩至极限。保持动作 1 秒后伸直双腿还原。（图 4-3-14）

Behavioral Essentials:

(1) Place your legs on the Swiss ball and use your arms support your body on the ground. Your arms are shoulder-width apart.

(2) Keep your upper body position unchanged and bend your legs forward so that the Swiss ball can roll forward under the ankle until the abdominal muscles contract to the limit. Hold for 1 second and then straighten your legs to restore. (Fig.4-3-14)

负荷强度：6 组，每组 12 次，每组间歇 60 秒。

Intensity: 6 sets in all, each set for 12 times, then taking a 60-second break.

注意事项：

（1）上体挺直，屈膝时应保持上体稳定。

（2）臀部保持稳定，不能塌陷或上翘。

Attentions:

(1) Keep the upper body straight and stable when bending your knees.

(2) Maintain stability of the buttocks, without collapsing or cocking up.

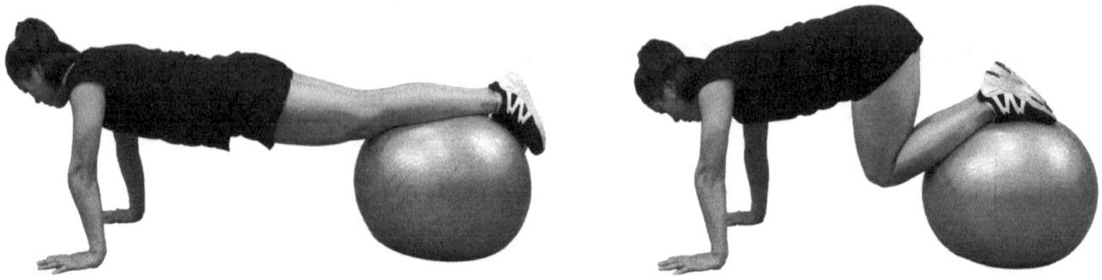

图 4–3–14 瑞士球屈腿内收

Fig.4–3–14 Bend your legs on the swiss ball

15. 瑞士球屈膝内收 Bend Your Knees on the Swiss Ball

锻炼部位：腹直肌、髂腰肌。

Muscles exercised: Rectus abdominis, iliopsoas.

动作要领：

（1）将双腿膝盖上方部位搭于瑞士球球面，双手与肩同宽支撑地面，呈俯卧姿势。

（2）收缩下腹肌，臀部尽可能向上，让瑞士球有控制地滚动到小腿的位置，让膝盖逐渐贴近胸部。

（3）将膝盖推回原位，放松腹肌，让瑞士球慢慢回到起始位置。（图 4-3-15）

Behavioral essentials:

(1) Place the upper part of the knees on the Swiss ball, and use your arms to support

your body on the ground. Your arms are shoulder-width apart in a prone position.

(2) Contact the lower abdominal muscles to make your buttock upward as far much possible. Control the Swiss ball rolling to your shanks and then move your knees gradually close to your chest.

(3) Push your knees back to the original position, relax the abdominal muscles, and then let the Swiss ball slowly roll back to the initial position. (Fig.4-3-15)

负荷强度：6 组，每组 12 次，每组间歇 60 秒。

Intensity: 6 sets in all, each set for 12 times, then taking a 60-second break.

注意事项：

（1）双手不能移动，要依靠腹肌发力完成动作。

（2）上体要挺直，腰背不能弯曲。

Attentions:

(1) Don't move your hands and it is necessary to rely on the abdominal muscles to complete the whole set of actions.

(2) Keep your upper body straight and don't bend.

图 4–3–15 瑞士球屈膝内收

Fig.4–3–15 Bend your knees on the swiss ball

16. 俯卧双腿支撑收腹 Contract Abdominal Muscles with Legs Supporting in the Prone Position

锻炼部位：三角肌、冈下肌、肱三头肌。

Muscles exercised: Deltoid, infraspinatus, triceps.

动作要领：

（1）双腿支撑在瑞士球球面上，双手与肩同宽支撑地面。

（2）直臂撑地，屈膝收腹，伸展腰腹，至起始位。（图 4-3-16）

Behavioral essentials:

(1) Place your legs on the Swiss ball, and use your arms to support your body on

the ground. Your arms are shoulder-width apart.

(2) Support your body with your forearms, draw your knees toward your chest to engage the core, then extend your hips and abdomen to retum to the starting position. (Fig.4-3-16)

负荷强度：6 组，每组 12 次，每组间歇 60 秒。

Intensity: 6 sets in all, each set for 12 times, then taking a 60-second break.

注意事项：

（1）屈膝收腹时要保持身体平衡。

（2）身体移动时瑞士球前后滚动。

Attentions:

(1) Keep your body balanced when bending your knees and contracting abdominal muscles.

(2) The Swiss ball should be rolled back and forth while the body moves.

图 4-3-16　俯卧双腿支撑收腹

Fig.4-3-16　Contract abdominal muscles with legs supporting in the prone position

17. 俯撑撞击弹回 Hit & Back with Arms Supporting in Prone Position

锻炼部位：腹直肌、腹外斜肌、腹内斜肌、腹横肌。

Muscles exercised: Rectus abdominis, external oblique, internal oblique, transverse abdominis.

动作要领：

（1）双臂支撑于瑞士球两侧，两脚分开与肩同宽，呈俯卧姿势。

（2）两臂伸直，双手突然离开平衡球，身体下降后胸部撞击球面，利用球面弹力弹回身体，两臂顺势支撑还原动作。（图 4-3-17）

Behavioral essentials:

(1) Put the arms on both sides of the Swiss ball, and two feet are separated with shoulder-width apart in a prone position.

(2) Keep the arms straight, and hands leave the balance ball suddenly. Descend the body to make your chest hit the balance ball. Then bounce the body back by the elasticity, and finally restore to the original position with your arms supporting the ground. (Fig.4-3-17)

负荷强度：3 组，每组 12 次，每组间歇 90 秒。

Intensity: 3 sets in all, each set for 12 times, then taking a 90-second break.

注意事项：

（1）动作过程中身体要挺直，头与颈要保持稳定。

（2）还原时双臂支撑于球面两侧，不能支撑于球面顶部。双臂应与肩同宽或略宽于肩。

（3）可以通过腿分开的距离来调整难度，双腿距离越小难度越大。

Attentions:

(1) Your body should be straight and your head and neck should be stable.

(2) When you restore, keep your arms on both sides of the ball which cannot be supported on the top of the ball. The arms should be shoulder width or slightly wider than that.

(3) The difficulty can be adjusted by separating your legs. The closer the legs are, the harder it is.

图 4–3–17 俯撑撞击弹回
Fig.4–3–17 Hit & back with arms supporting in prone position

18. 仰卧持球直臂转体 Twist Your Body with Straight Arms and Holding a Ball in Your Hands in Supine Position

锻炼部位：腹直肌、腹外斜肌、腹内斜肌、腹横肌。

Muscles exercised: Rectus abdominis, external oblique, internal oblique, transverse abdominis.

动作要领：

（1）躺在瑞士球球面上，上体与地面保持平行，大腿与小腿成 90° 夹角，双脚分开与肩同宽。双手持实心球于胸前，手臂向上挺直。

（2）持实心球向身体左右摆动，顺势转体，转体时要使肩部外侧贴到瑞士球

表面，随后还原向反方向摆动。（图 4-3-18）

Behavioral essentials:

(1) Lie on the Swiss ball,keep your upper body parallel to the ground. Your thighs should be at an angle of 90 degrees to your shank. Feet apart and shoulder are the same as wide. Hold a medicine ball over your chest and straighten your arms.

(2) Swing the medicine ball to the left and right of the body to twist your body. The outside of the shoulder should touch the surface of the Swiss ball when you twist.Then restore and swing to the opposite direction. (Fig.4-3-18)

负荷强度：3 组，每组 16 次，每组间歇 60 秒。

Intensity: 3 sets in all, each set for 16 times, then taking a 60-second break.

注意事项：

（1）核心要保持紧张，臀部不能下陷。

（2）双脚支撑要稳固，动作过程中瑞士球不能移动。

（3）实心球可以换成小重量的杠铃片或杠铃。

（4）头部、颈部要固定，不能仰头或低头。

Attentions:

(1) Keep your core tight and do not sink your hip.

(2) Your feet should be stable, and the Swiss ball cannot be moved when the action is completed.

(3) The machine ball can be replaced with a small weight barbell sheet or barbell.

(4) Your head and neck should be fixed and cannot be raised or lowered.

图 4-3-18　仰卧持球直臂转体

Fig.4-3-18　Twist your body with straight arms and holding a ball in your hands in supine position

19. 仰卧支撑提臀 Lift Your Hips in Supine Position

锻炼部位：股二头肌、半腱肌、半膜肌、臀大肌。

Muscles exercised: Biceps femoris, semitendinosus, semimembranosus, gluteus maximus.

动作要领：

（1）平躺在地，双脚蹬在瑞士球侧上方。动作开始时双腿支撑于瑞士球上，臀部抬离地面。

（2）双腿蹬直，当身体挺直成一条直线时稍微保持姿势，然后屈膝还原。（图 4-3-19）

Behavioral essentials:

(1) Lie on the ground, with your feet on top side of the Swiss ball. At the beginning, legs are supported by the Swiss ball and lift your hips off the ground.

(2) Straighten your legs, hold your posture for a while when your body is straight. Then bend your knees to restore. (Fig.4-3-19)

负荷强度：3 组，每组 12 次，每组间歇 60 秒。

Intensity：3 sets in all, each set for 12 times, then taking a 60-second break.

注意事项：

（1）保持腰部和臀部的紧张，使其不接触地面。

（2）保持动作时，双脚脚尖要朝上，身体挺直成一条直线，不能弯曲。

Attentions:

(1) Keep your waist and hips tight and do not touch the ground.

图 4–3–19　仰卧支撑提臀
Fig.4–3–19　Lift your hips in supine position

(2) When you hold the posture, keep tiptoes upwards and straighten your body which cannot be bent.

20. 倚球支撑蹲伸 Leaning on the Ball to Support Squatting and Stretching

锻炼部位：股四头肌、腹直肌、胫骨前肌

Muscles exercised: Quadriceps femoris, rectus abdominis, tibialis anterior

动作要领：

（1）坐立于瑞士球球面上，随后身体下移，双手贴腰，腰部和背部贴到球面

侧上方，双脚蹬直并分离，距离与肩同宽，脚跟支撑于地面。

（2）屈膝，身体沿平衡球面下滑。稍微保持动作后蹬膝还原。

Behavioral essentials:

(1) Sit on the Swiss ball, then move down the body with your hands firmly on your waist. Let your waist and back attach to the front side of the ball. Keep your legs straight and your feet shoulder-width apart.Use your heels to support your body.

(2) Bend your knees and make your body slide down along the surface of the swiss ball. Hold the position briefly, then extend your legs to return to the starting position.

负荷强度：3 组，每组 12 次，每组间歇 60 秒。

Intensity: 3 sets in all, each set for 12 times, then taking a 60-second break.

注意事项：

（1）要用脚后跟支撑地面，支撑时保持核心紧张，上体挺直。

（2）下蹲时动作要缓慢。

（3）可以通过缩小双脚间的距离增加难度，距离越小则难度越大。

Attentions:

(1) Support the ground with your heels.Keep the core tight and the upper body straight.

(2) When squatting, move slowly.

(3) You can increase the difficulty by reducing the distance between your feet. The smaller the distance, the more difficult it is.

图 4-3-20　倚球支撑蹲伸

Fig.4-3-20　Leaning on the ball to support squatting and stretching

21. 瑞士球仰卧起坐 Sit-up on a Swiss Ball

锻炼部位：竖脊肌、菱形肌、腹直肌、多裂肌。

Muscles exercised: Erector spinae, rhomboideus, rectus abdominis, multifidus.

动作要领：

（1）双手两肘外展抱头坐于瑞士球前上方，大腿与小腿成 90° 夹角支撑于地面。

（2）上体沿瑞士球上部后仰，头尽量向下贴近瑞士球球面，随后收腹还原坐立。（图 4-3-21）

Behavioral essentials:

(1) Extend both elbows with both hands and sit in front of the Swiss ball, holding your head and supporting your thighs and calves at a 90° angle on the ground.

(2) Lean the upper body back along the Swiss ball, and make the head as close as possible to the Swiss ball.Then crunch and sit up to restore. (Fig.4-3-21)

负荷强度：3 组，每组 12 次，每组间歇 60 秒。

Intensity: 3 sets in all, each set for 12 times, then taking a 60-second break.

注意事项：

（1）双脚支撑要稳，动作过程中瑞士球不能移动。

（2）上体仰卧和直立过程中动作要缓慢，下一次动作不能借助上一次动作的惯性。

Attentions:

(1) Your supporting feet should be stable, and the Swiss ball cannot be moved.

(2) During the process of lying down and standing upright, the movement should be slow, and the next movement should not rely on the inertia of the previous movement.

图 4–3–21 瑞士球仰卧起坐

Fig.4–3–21 Sit–up on a Swiss ball

22. 瑞士球俯卧背起 V-ups by Lying Prostrate on a Swiss Ball

锻炼部位：竖脊肌、臀大肌。

Muscles exercised: Erector spinae, gluteus maximus.

动作要领：

（1）腹部和胸部贴于瑞士球顶部，双手抱头，两腿伸直，脚尖支撑于地面。

（2）上体抬起直立，当上体与地面达到或接近垂直时稍微保持动作，随后下放还原。（图 4-3-22）

Behavioral essentials:

(1) Keep your abdomen and chest attached to the top of the Swiss ball with hands on your head. Straighten your legs and use tiptoes to support your body on the ground.

(2) Lift your upper body up-right, and hold the pose for a while when the upper body is nearly vertical to the ground. Then restore. (Fig.4-3-22)

负荷强度：3 组，每组 12 次，每组间歇 60 秒。

Intensity: 3 sets in all, each set for 12 times, then taking a 60-second break.

注意事项：

（1）保证双脚支撑稳定，动作过程中瑞士球不能移动。

（2）还原俯卧时动作要缓慢。

（3）动作过程中保持头部、颈部的稳定。

Attentions:

(1) Ensure that your supporting feet are stable. The Swiss ball cannot be moved.

(2) Move slowly when restore.

(3) Keep the head and neck stable.

图 4-3-22 瑞士球俯卧背起

Fig.4-3-22 V-ups by lying prostrate on a Swiss ball

23. 瑞士球俯拜 Swiss Ball Prone Bow

锻炼部位： 臀大肌、腹直肌、竖脊肌。

Muscles exercised: Gluteus maximus, rectus abdominis, erector spinae.

动作要领：

（1）俯卧在瑞士球上，上体与下体形成夹角夹住瑞士球。

（2）身体发力，双手向前伸直扶住地面，同时双腿向后蹬伸抬起。稍微保持姿势后还原。（图 4-3-23）

Behavioral essentials:

(1) Face down on the Swiss ball, make your upper body and lower body form an angle to grip the Swiss ball.

(2) Use the power from your body to support yourself with your hands straight forward on the ground. At the same time, raise your legs straight back.Hold the posture for a while and then restore. (Fig.4-3-23)

负荷强度： 3 组，每组 12 次，每组间歇 60 秒。

Intensity: 3 sets in all, each set for 12 times, then taking a 60-second break.

注意事项：

（1）动作过程中保持球面稳定，瑞士球不能移动。

（2）蹬伸时身体要保持挺直，成一条直线。

Attentions:

(1) Keep the Swiss ball stable and do not move it.

(2) Keep your body straight and stretch in a straight line.

图 4-3-23　瑞士球俯拜

Fig.4-3-23　Swiss ball prone bow

24. 俯撑前后滑动 Slide Forward or Backward by Lying Prostrate on a Swiss Ball

锻炼部位：三角肌、肱三头肌、冈上肌。

Muscles exercised: Deltoid, triceps muscle of arm, supraspinatus.

动作要领：

（1）上体俯卧在瑞士球上，双脚用力蹬地，身体沿瑞士球向前滑动。

（2）双手撑地缓冲，同时双腿蹬伸，与躯干成一条直线。稍微保持姿势后双手撑地向后滑动还原。（图 4-3-24）

Behavioral essentials:

(1) Lie your upper body on the Swiss ball with both feet on the ground.Then slide the body forward along the Swiss ball.

(2) The hands are supported by the ground, while stretch your legs in a line with the trunk. After holding the posture for a while, slide backward with your hands to restore. (Fig.4-3-24)

负荷强度：3 组，每组 12 次，每组间歇 60 秒。

Intensity: 3 sets in all, each set for 12 times, then taking a 60-second break.

注意事项：

（1）在进行动作时，胸部和腹部要紧贴在球面上保持平衡。

（2）蹬伸后身体应保持成一条直线，双腿不能弯曲。

Attentions:

(1) Keep your chest and abdomen close to the surface of the Swiss ball to maintain balance.

(2) After stretching, the body should be kept in a straight line and the legs should not be bent.

图 4–3–24　俯撑前后滑动

Fig.4–3–24　Slide forward or backward by lying prostrate on a Swiss ball

25. 俯撑前滚屈肘 Bend Your Elbows by Rolling the Swiss Ball Forward

锻炼部位：肱三头肌、腹直肌。

Muscles exercised: Triceps, rectus abdominis.

动作要领：

（1）双手支撑在瑞士球上，躯干倾斜，双脚脚尖支撑地面，身体挺直。

（2）双臂屈肘向前滚球，当肘部和前臂支撑在球面上时伸肘还原。（图 4-3-25）

Behavioral essentials:

(1) Put your hands on the Swiss ball and incline your body. Then use your tiptoes to support your body and keep your body straight.

(2) Bend your elbows to roll the Swiss ball forwards. Restore your elbows when your elbows and forearms are touching the ball. (Fig.4-3-25)

负荷强度：3 组，每组 12 次，每组间歇 90 秒。

Intensity: 3 sets in all, each set for 12 times, then taking a 90-second break.

注意事项：

（1）进行动作时核心部位要保持紧张，身体要稳定，始终成一条直线。

（2）屈肘下降时速度要缓慢。

Attentions:

(1) Keep your core tight and your body should be stable and always in a straight line.

(2) It should be slowly when you lower the elbows.

图 4–3–25 俯撑前滚屈肘

Fig.4–3–25 Bend your elbows by rolling the Swiss ball forward

26. 四点支撑平衡练习 Balancing Exercise by Four-point Supporting

锻炼部位：腹直肌、腹横肌、多裂肌。

Muscles exercised: Rectus abdominis, transversus abdominis, multifidus.

动作要领：

（1）双腿搭在瑞士球球面上，双手支撑地面，成俯卧撑姿势。

（2）屈膝收小腿，双手向后爬行逐渐靠近瑞士球。

（3）接近瑞士球后单手离开地面扶住瑞士球，待身体平衡后另一只手也离开地面扶住瑞士球，在球面上双手与双膝形成四个平衡点。（图 4-3-26）

Behavioral essentials:

(1) Put your legs on the Swiss ball and use your hands support your body on the ground in a prone position.

(2) Bend your knees and crawl back with both hands to approach the Swiss ball.

(3) After approaching the Swiss ball, one hand leave the ground to hold the Swiss ball. After your body is balanced, the other hand also should leave the ground to hold the Swiss ball. Your hands and knees would be the four balanced points on the ball. (Fig.4-3-26)

负荷强度：三组，每组坚持平衡姿势 12 秒，每组间歇 60 秒。

Intensity: 3 sets in all, each set for 12 second, then taking a 60-second break.

注意事项：

（1）移动过程要缓慢。

（2）保持姿势稳定，上体不能晃动。

Attentions:

(1) Move slowly.

(2) Keep the posture stable and do not waggle your upper body.

图 4–3–26　四点支撑平衡练习

Fig.4–3–26　Balancing exercise by four–point supporting

CHAPTER 5

第五章

核心力量复合器械训练

Core Strength Training with Complex Instruments

第一节　瑞士球组合训练

Section 1　Swiss Ball Training

1. 瑞士球支撑收腹 Crunch with Swiss Ball Support

锻炼部位： 腹直肌。

Muscles exercised: Rectus abdominis.

动作要领：

（1）收腹臀部将瑞士球前滚。

（2）手臂支撑位置保持稳定。（图 5-1-1）

Behavioral essentials:

(1) Roll the Swiss ball forwards as you make the crunch.

(2) Keep your arms support position stable. (Fig.5-1-1)

负荷强度： 3 组，每组 12 次，每组间歇 15 秒。

Intensity: 3 sets in all, each set for 12 times, then taking a 15-second break.

注意事项：

（1）始终绷紧腹部。

（2）背部微微拱起。

（3）掌跟发力支持，保持稳定。

Attentions:

(1) Keep your abdomen tightened.

(2) Your back is slightly arched.

(3) Stay stable and your hands will

图 5-1-1　瑞士球支撑收腹

Fig.5-1-1　Crunch with Swiss ball support

support the body.

2. 瑞士球跪姿收腹 Kneeling Crunch with Swiss Ball

锻炼部位： 臀大肌、竖脊肌。

Muscles exercised: Gluteus maximus, erector spinae.

动作要领：

（1）手臂始终压住瑞士球，不能耸肩。

（2）感受腹部发力。

（3）身体前倾将瑞士球向前滚动，滚至腹肌能承受的最大幅度。

（4）收腹弯腰，将瑞士球拉回。

（5）还原时呼吸，滚至最远时憋气。（图 5-1-2）

Behavioral essentials:

(1) Press the Swiss ball with your arms and do not shrug.

(2) Use the force from the abdomen.

(3) Roll the Swiss ball forward as your body lean forwards. Roll forwards as far as your abdominal muscles can handle.

(4) Bend your waist and make crunch to pull the Swiss ball back.

(5) Breathe when you roll the ball back, and hold your breath as you roll to the farthest position. (Fig.5-1-2)

负荷强度： 3 组，每组 12 次，每组间歇 15 秒。

Intensity: 3 sets in all, each set for 12 times, then taking a 15-second break.

注意事项：

（1）先收腹，再收回手臂。

（2）腹部收缩发力。

Attentions:

(1) Make crunch first and take the arm back.

(2) Use the force from abdominal.

图 5-1-2　瑞士球跪姿收腹

Fig.5-1-2　Kneeling crunch with Swiss ball

3. 瑞士球反向卷腹 Reverse Crunch with Swiss Ball

锻炼部位：腹直肌、腹横肌、腹外斜肌、髂腰肌。

Muscles exercised: Rectus abdominis, transversus abdominis, external oblique muscle, iliopsoas.

动作要领：

（1）双腿膝盖夹紧瑞士球。

（2）抬腿时臀部离开地面。

（3）下落时瑞士球不能触地。

（4）还原时吸气，抬腿时呼气。（图 5-1-3）

Behavioral essentials:

(1) Clamp the Swiss ball with your knees.

(2) Your hips leave the ground as you lift your legs.

(3) The Swiss ball can't touch the ground when it goes down.

(4) Inhale when you return to the start position and exhale when the legs are lifted. (Fig.5-1-3)

负荷强度：3 组，每组 12 次，每组间歇 15 秒。

Intensity: 3 sets in all, each set for 12 times, then taking a 15-second break.

注意事项：

（1）减慢速度，不能让动作带有惯性。

（2）腰部始终是放松状态。

Attentions:

(1) Slow down, you can't make the movement with inertia.

(2) Your waist is always relaxed.

图 5–1–3　瑞士球反向卷腹

Fig.5–1–3　Reverse crunch with Swiss ball

4. 瑞士球转体卷腹 Rotation with Swiss Ball

锻炼部位：腹直肌、腹横肌、腹外斜肌。

Muscles exercised: Rectus abdominis, transverses abdominis, external oblique muscle.

动作要领：

（1）腰部贴地，双手夹紧瑞士球。

（2）卷腹起身，将瑞士球移到大腿侧面。

（3）还原时吸气，卷腹时呼气。

（4）卷腹时，腹肌沿斜对角方向有挤压感。（图 5-1-4）

Behavioral essentials:

(1) Keep your waist attached to the ground, and the Swiss ball is clamped with both hands.

(2) Crunch up and move the Swiss ball to the sides of the thighs.

(3) Inhale when you return to the start position and exhale when you make crunch.

(4) When you make crunch, the abdominal muscles have a sense of extrusion along the diagonal direction. (Fig.5-1-4)

负荷强度：3 组，每组 12 次（左右两侧向算一次），每组间歇 15 秒。

Intensity: 3 sets in all, each set for 12 times（both sides count as 1 time）, then taking a 15-second break.

注意事项：

（1）减慢速度。

（2）感受腹部发力。

（3）腰部不能离开地面。

Attentions:

(1)Slow down.

(2)Use the force from the abdomen.

(3)Your waist can't leave the ground.

图 5–1–4　瑞士球转体卷腹

Fig.5–1–4　Rotation with Swiss ball

5. 瑞士球仰卧递球 Pass the Swiss Ball in a Supine Gesture

锻炼部位：腹直肌、腹横肌、腹外斜肌、髂腰肌。

Muscles exercised: Rectus abdominis, transversus abdominis, external oblique muscle, iliopsoas.

动作要领：

（1）下背部紧贴地面。

（2）手臂、双腿绷紧。

（3）摆动时不能放松膝关节和肘关节。

（4）递球时呼气，下放时吸气。（图 5-1-5）

Behavioral essentials:

(1) Keep your lower back toughing the ground.

(2) Tight your arms and legs.

(3) Your knee joints and elbow joints can not be relaxed when swinging.

(4) Inhale when you pass the ball, and exhale when you put it down. (Fig.5-1-5)

负荷强度：3 组，每组 12 次，每组间歇 15 秒。

Intensity: 3 sets in all, each set for 12 times, then taking a 15-second break.

注意事项：

（1）双臂、双腿伸直，绷紧。

（2）腹部始终保持紧绷。

（3）保持腰部贴地。

Attentions:

(1) Both arms and legs are stretched and tightened.

(2) Keep your abdomen tight.

(3) Keep your waist touching the ground.

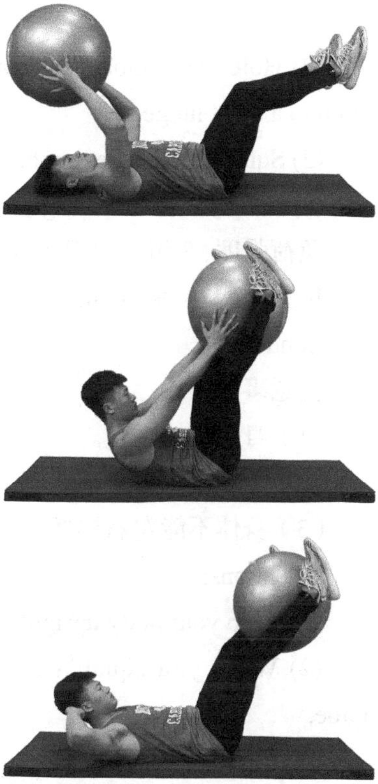

图 5-1-5 瑞士球仰卧递球
Fig.5-1-5 Pass the Swiss ball in a supine gesture

6. 瑞士球弓步哑铃蹲起 Lunge Squat with Dumbbell and Swiss Ball

锻炼部位：三角肌、腹直肌。

Muscles exercised: Deltoid, rectus abdominis.

动作要领：

（1）目视前方。

（2）两手持哑铃，一条腿撑于瑞士球上成前弓步。

（3）下蹲同时上举哑铃。

（4）躯干保持正直。（图 5-1-6）

Behavioral essentials:

(1) Look ahead.

(2) Hole the dumbbell in both hands. The hind leg is supported on the Swiss ball and into a front lunge.

(3) Squat and lift the dumbbell in your hands.

(4) Keep your torso upright. (Fig.5-1-6)

负荷强度：3 组，每组 12 次，每组间歇 15 秒。

Intensity: 3 sets in all, each set for 12 times, then taking a 15-second break.

注意事项：

（1）身体保持正直。

（2）下蹲时膝关节不要超过脚尖。

（3）身体不能左右摇摆。

Attentions:

(1) Keep your body upright.

(2) When you squat, your knees can not exceed your tiptoe.

(3) Your body can not swing.

图 5–1–6 瑞士球弓步哑铃蹲起
Fig.5–1–6 Lunge squat with dumbbell and Swiss ball

7. 仰卧瑞士球哑铃飞 Lying Supine Swiss Ball Dumbbell Flying

锻炼部位：腹直肌、腹横肌。

Muscles exercised: Rectus abdominis, transversus abdominis.

动作要领：

（1）仰卧在瑞士球上。

（2）两脚开立与肩同宽，上体与大腿保持在同一水平面上。

（3）两手各握一哑铃，两臂伸直置于身体两侧。

（4）两臂上举靠近身体中线。（图 5-1-7）

Behavioral essentials:

(1) Lying on the Swiss ball.

(2) The feet are shoulder-width apart.Keep your upper body at the same level as thighs.

(3) Hold a dumbbell in each hand and keep your arms straight at your sides.

(4) Raise both arms close to the midline of the body. (Fig.5-1-7)

负荷强度：3 组，每组 12 次，每组间歇 15 秒。

Intensity: 3 sets in all, each set for 12 times, then taking a 15-second break.

注意事项：

（1）上体挺直。

（2）腰、腹部收紧。

（3）两臂伸直。

Attentions:

(1) Keep your upper body straight.

(2) Tighten your waist and abdomen.

(3) Keep your arms straight.

图 5–1–7 仰卧瑞士球哑铃飞

Fig.5–1–7 Lying supine Swiss ball dumbbell flying

8. 瑞士球上负重体屈伸 Weight-bearing Body Kip on Swiss Ball

锻炼部位：竖脊肌。

Muscles exercised: Erector spinae.

动作要领：

（1）坐在瑞士球上，两手握杠铃于肩上。

（2）上体挺直，两脚开立与肩同宽。

（3）上体前倾与地面平行。稍微保持姿态后还原。（图 5-1-8）

Behavioral essentials：

(1) Sit on a Swiss ball and hold the barbell on your shoulders.

(2) Keep your upper body straight, and your feet are shoulder-width apart.

(3) The upper body lean forward to parallel to the ground. Hold the posture for a while and then restore. (Fig.5-1-8)

负荷强度：3 组，每组 12 次，每组间歇 15 秒。

Intensity: 3 sets in all, each set for 12 times, then taking a 15-second break.

注意事项：

（1）胸、背、腹部收紧。

（2）腰部发力保持平衡。

Attentions:

(1) Tighten your chest, back and abdomen.

(2) Use your waist strength to maintain balance.

图 5–1–8　瑞士球上负重体屈伸

Fig.5–1–8　Weight–bearing body kip on Swiss ball

9. 瑞士球上负重转体 Weight-bearing Body Rotation on Swiss Ball

锻炼部位：腹外斜肌、下后锯肌。

Muscles exercised: Ventral oblique muscle, serratus posterior inferior.

动作要领：

（1）坐在瑞士球上，两手握杠铃于肩上。

（2）上体挺直，两脚开立与肩同宽。

（3）上体向一侧转动，左右两侧交替进行。（图 5-1-9）

Behavioral essentials:

(1) Sit on a Swiss ball, hold the barbell on your shoulders.

(2) Keep your upper body straight and your feet shoulder-width apart.

(3) The upper body rotates to left and right sides alternately. (Fig.5-1-9)

负荷强度：训练 3 组，每组 12 次，每组间歇 15 秒。

Intensity: 3 sets in all, each set for 12 times, then taking a 15-second break.

注意事项：

（1）胸、背、腹部收紧。

（2）腰部发力保持平衡。

Attentions:

(1) Tighten your chest, back and abdomen.

(2) Use your waist strength to maintain balance.

图 5-1-9　瑞士球上负重转体

Fig.5-1-9　Weight-bearing body rotation on Swiss ball

10. 瑞士球上卧推 Push on the Swiss Ball

锻炼部位：胸大肌、胸小肌、三头肌、腹直肌、腹横肌、竖脊肌。

Muscles exercised: Pectoralis major, pectoralis minor, triceps, rectus abdominis, transversus abdominis, erector spinae.

动作要领：

（1）仰卧，背部支撑于瑞士球上。

（2）两脚开立与肩同宽。

（3）两手握杠铃于胸前，向上推举。（图 5-1-10）

Behavioral essentials:

(1) Lie on your back and support yourself on the Swiss ball.

(2) The feet are shoulder-width apart.

(3) Hold the barbell in both hands over your chest and push up. (Fig.5-1-10)

负荷强度：3 组，每组 12 次，每组间歇 15 秒。

Intensity: 3 sets in all, each set for 12 times, then taking a 15-second break.

注意事项：

（1）腰部发力收紧。

（2）臀部夹紧。

（3）两臂距离与肩同宽。

Attentions:

(1) Tighten your waist.

(2) Keep your buttocks clamped.

(3) Arms are as wide as shoulders

图 5-1-10 瑞士球上卧推

Fig.5-1-10 Push on the Swiss ball

11. 瑞士球弓步负重蹲起 Weighted Lunges Squat with Swiss Ball

锻炼部位：股四头肌、腹直肌。

Muscles exercised: Quadriceps femoris, rectus abdominis

动作要领：

（1）目视前方。

（2）后腿撑于瑞士球上成前弓步。

（3）双手持杠铃下蹲。

（4）躯干保持正直。（图 5-1-11）

Behavioral essentials:

(1) Keep looking ahead.

(2) The hind leg is on the Swiss ball and do lunge.

(3) Squat with barbell on both hands.

(4) Keep your trunk upright. (Fig.5-1-11)

负荷强度：3 组，每组 12 次，每组间歇 15 秒。

Intensity: 3 sets in all, each set for 12 times, then taking a 15-second break.

注意事项：

（1）身体保持正直。

（2）下蹲时膝关节不要超过脚尖。

图 5-1-11 瑞士球弓步负重蹲起

Fig.5-1-11 Weighted lunges squat with Swiss ball

（3）身体不能左右晃动。

Attentions:

(1) Keep your body upright.

(2) Your knee can not go over your tiptoe when you bend your knee.

(3) Your body can not swing.

12. 瑞士球俯卧后抬腿 Lie Prost-rate and Lift Legs on the Swiss ball

锻炼部位：臀大肌。

Muscles exercised: Gluteus maximus.

动作要领：

（1）瑞士球位于腹部下方，双手支撑于地面。

（2）双腿并拢，勾起脚尖，用力绷直。

（3）抬腿时呼吸，还原时吸气。（图 5-1-12）

Behavioral essentials:

(1) The Swiss ball is located underneath the abdomen with both hands on the ground.

(2) Bring your legs together, lift your tiptoes, and use force to straighten them.

(3) Exhale when you lift legs, inhale when you release. (Fig.5-1-12)

负荷强度：3 组，每组 12 次，每组间歇 15 秒。

Intensity: 3 sets in all, each set for 12 times, then taking a 15-second break.

注意事项：

（1）腹部收紧。

（2）控制双腿抬起的高度。

（3）掌根发力支撑，保持稳定。

Attention:

(1) Tighten your abdomen.

(2) Control the height of your legs.

(3) Use your palm to support your body and keep stable.

图 5–1–12 瑞士球俯卧后抬腿
Fig.5–1–12 Lie prostrate and lift legs on the Swiss ball

13. 肘撑瑞士球后踢腿 Calf Raises with Your Elbows on Swiss Ball

锻炼部位：臀大肌、腹直肌、腹横肌。

Muscles exercised: Gluteus maximus, rectus abdominis,transversus abdominis.

动作要领：

（1）俯卧，两臂屈肘支撑于瑞士球上。

（2）两腿伸直支撑于地面。

（3）一侧腿向后摆，两腿交替进行。（图 5-1-13）

Behavioral essentials:

(1) Lie prostrate and bend your elbows on Swiss ball.

(2) Legs are stretched and supported on the ground.

(3) Swing every leg backward alternately. (Fig.5-1-13)

负荷强度：3 组，每组 12 次，每组间歇 15 秒。

Intensity: 3 sets in all, each set for 12 times, then taking a 15-second break.

注意事项：

（1）胸、腹、背部收紧。

（2）膝关节伸直。

（3）臀部夹紧。

Attentions:

(1) Tighten your chest, abdomen and back.

(2) Tighten your knee joints.

(3) Clamp your buttocks.

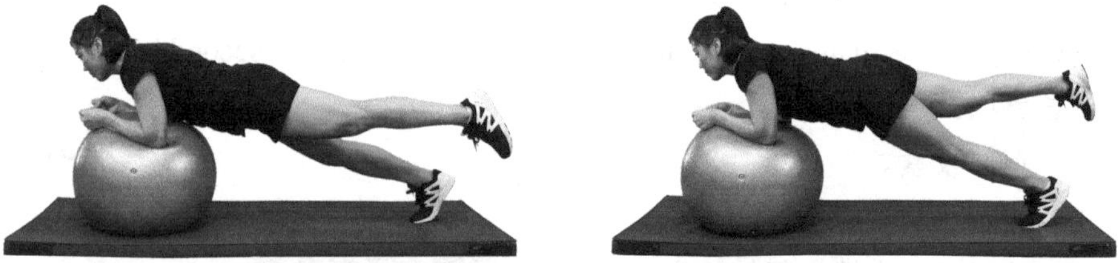

图 5-1-13 肘撑瑞士球后踢腿

Fig.5-1-13 Calf raises with your elbows on Swiss ball

14. 肘撑瑞士球斜后踢腿 Calf Raises Slantingly with Your Elbows on Swiss Ball

锻炼部位：臀中肌、臀小肌、腹直肌、腹横肌。

Muscles exercised: Medius gluteus, gluteus minimus, rectus abdominis, transversus abdominis.

动作要领：

（1）俯卧，两臂屈肘支撑于瑞士球上。

（2）两腿并拢伸直支撑于地面。

（3）一侧腿向斜后方摆，两腿交替进行。（图 5-1-14）

Behavioral essentials:

(1) Lie prostrate and bend your elbows on Swiss ball.

(2) Legs are tied together and supported on the ground.

(3) Slantingly swing every leg backward alternately. (Fig.5-1-14)

负荷强度：3 组，每组 12 次，每组间歇 15 秒。

Intensity: 3 sets in all, each set for 12 times, then taking a 15-second break.

注意事项：

（1）腰、腹、背部收紧。

（2）膝关节伸直。

（3）髋关节固定。

Attentions:

(1) Tighten your waist, abdomen and back.

(2) Straightening your knee joints.

(3) Fix your hip joints.

图 5–1–14 肘撑瑞士球斜后踢腿

Fig.5–1–14 Calf raises slantingly with your elbows on Swiss ball

15. 仰卧瑞士球向上踢腿 Kick Up by Lying Supine on Swiss Ball

锻炼部位：腹直肌。

Muscles exercised: Rectus abdominis.

动作要领：

（1）仰卧，背部压在瑞士球上。

（2）两脚开立与肩同宽，上体与大腿保持在同一水平面。

（3）两手扶于球两侧。

（4）一侧腿伸直向上踢，两腿交替进行。（图 5-1-15）

Behavioral essentials:

(1) Lying supine. Press your back against the Swiss ball .

(2) Your feet are shoulder-width apart, and your upper body and thighs are kept in the same horizontal plane.

(3) Place both hands on either side of the ball.

(4) Kick your legs straight up one by one alternately. (Fig.5-1-15)

负荷强度：3 组，每组 12 次，每组间歇 15 秒。

Intensity: 3 sets in all, each set for 12 times, then taking a 15-second break.

注意事项：

（1）上踢腿时膝关节伸直绷紧。

（2）髋部固定，不要晃动。

Attentions:

(1) Stretch your knee joints when you kick.

(2) Fix your hip, do not swing.

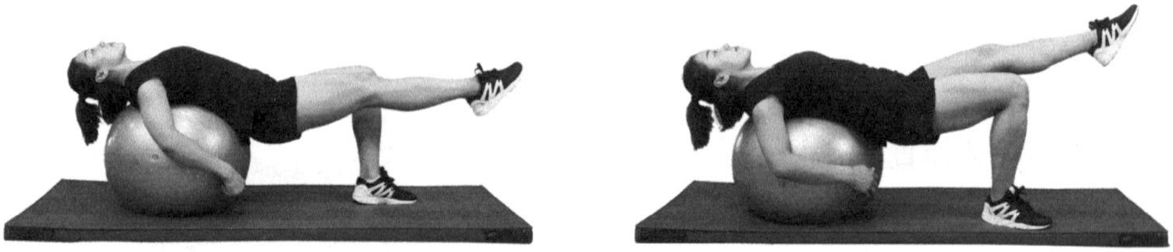

图 5-1-15　仰卧瑞士球向上踢腿

Fig.5-1-15　Kick up by lying supine on Swiss ball

第二节　弹力带组合训练

Section 2　Resistance Band Combination Training

1. 平衡盘弓步绳索划船 Balance Board Rowing

锻炼部位：背阔肌、腹直肌、腹横肌。

Muscles exercised: Latissimus dorsi, rectus abdominis, transversus abdominis.

动作要领：

（1）单脚站于平衡盘上呈弓步。

（2）后腿屈膝，重心在两腿之间。

（3）做单臂划船动作。

（4）呼气向后拉，吸气向前。（图 5-2-1）

Behavioral essentials:

(1) Stand on the balance board with one foot and do lunges.

(2) Bend your hind leg, knee and keep your center of gravity between your legs.

(3) Row on one arm.

(4) Exhale backward and inhale forward. (Fig.5-2-1)

负荷强度：3 组，每组 12 次，每组间歇 15 秒。

图 5-2-1　平衡盘弓步绳索划船
Fig.5-2-1　Balance board rowing

Intensity: 3 sets in all, each set for 12 times, then taking a 15-second break.

注意事项：

（1）身体保持直立。

（2）不能旋转或摇摆。

Attentions:

(1) Keep your body upright.

(2) Can not rotate or swing.

2. 弹力带平衡盘身体侧拉 Body Side Stretch with Resistance Band and Balance Board

锻炼部位：腹直肌、腹内斜肌、腹外斜肌、竖脊肌。

Muscles exercised: Rectus abdominis, obliquus internus abdominis, external oblique abdominal muscles, erector spinae.

动作要领：

（1）两脚前后开立，屈膝站立于平衡盘上。

（2）两臂伸直，两手头顶握紧弹力带。

（3）直臂向体侧屈体，直立还原。

（4）两侧交替进行。（图 5-2-2）

Behavioral essentials:

(1) Stand on the balance plate with your feet apart, bending your knees.

(2) Straighten your arms and keep your hands clenching the resistance band above your head.

(3) Keep your arms straight and do lateral flexion.Then return to upright position.

(4) Alternate on both sides. (Fig.5-2-2)

负荷强度：3 组，每组 12 次，每组间歇 15 秒。

Intensity: 3 sets in all, each set for 12 times, then taking a 15-second break.

注意事项：

（1）保持躯干固定。

（2）背部保持紧绷、直立。

（3）手臂伸直。

Attention:

(1) Keep your trunk fixed.

(2) Keep your back tight and upright.

(3) Straighten your arms.

图 5-2-2 弹力带平衡盘身体侧拉

Fig.5-2-2 Body side stretch with resistance band and balance board

3. 平衡盘单手侧支撑拉弹力带 Stretch Resistance Band with Single Hand Side Supporting on Balance Board

锻炼部位：三角肌、斜方肌、三头肌、腹外斜肌。

Muscles exercised: Deltoid, trapezius, triceps, external oblique abdominal muscles.

动作要领：

（1）一侧手臂伸直支撑于地面。

（2）将弹力带一端固定于支撑手掌下。

（3）两脚支撑于平衡盘上。

（4）未支撑手紧握弹力带将其向上方打开。

（5）保持两臂伸直处于一条直线，两臂交替进行。（图 5-2-3）

Behavioral essentials:

(1) One arm are stretched out to support on the ground.

(2) Fix one end of the resistance band under the supporting palm.

(3) Stand with your feet on the balance board.

(4) Use the other hand to hold the resistance band and stretch it upwards.

(5) Keep your arms straight in a line and do it alternately. (Fig.5-2-3)

负荷强度：3 组，每组 12 次，每组间歇 15 秒。

Intensity: 3 sets in all, each set for 12 times, then taking a 15-second break.

注意事项：

（1）身体成一条直线。

（2）膝关节伸直。

（3）手臂打开时伸直。

Attentions:

(1) Keep your body in a straight line.

(2) Straighten your knee joints.

(3) Straighten your arms when you stretch the resistance band upwards.

图 5–2–3　平衡盘单手侧支撑拉弹力带

Fig.5–2–3　Stretch resistance band with single hand side supporting on balance board

4. 瑞士球坐姿斜拉 Oblique Extension in Sitting Position on Swiss Ball

锻炼部位：腹外斜肌。

Muscles exercised: External oblique abdominal muscles.

动作要领：

（1）坐于瑞士球上，躯干与地面垂直，大小腿成 90°　。

（2）双手微屈肘在体侧，紧握弹力带。

（3）向斜上方拉弹力带至最大幅度。

（4）呼气向后拉，吸气还原。（图 5-2-4）

Behavioral essentials:

(1) Sit on a Swiss ball. Keep your torso perpendicular to the ground, and legs bend at 90 ° .

(2) Hold the resistance band with your elbows slightly bent on the side of your body.

(3) Stretch the resistance band as far as you can ramp above.

(4) Stretch after exhalation and inhale when you release. (Fig.5-2-4)

负荷强度：3 组，每组 12 次，每组间歇 15 秒。

Intensity: 3 sets in all, each set for 12 times, then taking a 15-second break.

注意事项：

（1）臀部紧贴瑞士球。

（2）身体保持平衡。

Attention:

(1) Keep your hips touching the Swiss ball.

(2) Keep your body balance.

图 5-2-4　瑞士球坐姿斜拉

Fig.5-2-4　Oblique extension in sitting position on Swiss ball

5. 瑞士球坐姿单臂后拉 Stretch One Arm Backward Sitting on Swiss Ball

锻炼部位：腹直肌、腹横肌、腹外斜肌、背阔肌。

Muscles exercised: Rectus abdominis, transversus abdominis, external oblique abdominal muscles, latissimus dorsi.

动作要领：

（1）坐于瑞士球上，上体稍后仰。

（2）一脚平放于地面，另一脚平抬起。

（3）保持坐姿，做单臂划船。

（4）呼气向后拉，吸气向前。（图 5-2-5）

Behavioral essentials:

(1) Sit on the Swiss ball slightly rearwards.

(2) Place one foot flat on the ground and lift the other foot flat.

(3) Keep sitting position and do single arm rowing.

(4) Exhale when you stretch and inhale when you release. (Fig.5-2-5)

负荷强度：3 组，每组 12 次，每组间歇 15 秒。

Intensity: 3 sets in all, each set for 12 times, then taking a 15-second break.

注意事项：

（1）保持身体姿势。

（2）身体勿来回摇摆。

Attentions:

(1) Keep good posture.

(2) Do not swing.

图 5-2-5 瑞士球坐姿单臂后拉

Fig.5-2-5 Stretch one arm backward sitting on Swiss ball

6. 瑞士球 + 弹力带转体侧拉 Twist and Side Stretch with Swiss Ball & Elastic Band

锻炼部位：腹内斜肌、腹外斜肌。

Muscles exercised: Obliquus internus abdominis, external oblique abdominal muscles.

动作要领：

（1）坐于瑞士球上，两脚自然分开。

（2）屈臂，两手紧握弹力带。

（3）向身体一侧转体侧拉。

（4）身体转正还原，两侧交替进行。（图 5-2-6）

Behavioral essentials:

(1) Sit on a Swiss ball with two feet naturally separated.

(2) Bend your elbows and hold the resistance band tightly in your hands.

(3) Twist and side stretch to one side.

(4) Your body covers to normal position, and do it alternately. (Fig.5-2-6)

负荷强度：3 组，每组 12 次，每组间歇 15 秒。

Intensity: 3 sets in all, each set for 12 times, then taking a 15-second break.

注意事项：

（1）保持躯干固定。

（2）腰、背部保持紧绷、直立。

Attentions:

(1) Keep your trunk fixed.

(2) Keep your waist and back tight and upright.

图 5-2-6 瑞士球 + 弹力带转体侧拉

Fig.5-2-6 Twist and side stretch with Swiss ball & elastic band

第三节 平衡盘组合训练

Section 3 Balance Board Combination Training

1. 平衡盘上侧平举 Flat Lifting on the Upper Side of the Balance Plate

锻炼部位：腹横肌、三角肌、斜方肌。

Muscles exercised: Transversus abdominis, deltoid, trapezius

动作要领：

（1）两脚开立，站于平衡盘上。

（2）背部挺直，两手各握一哑铃置于体侧。

（3）直臂侧平举。（图 5-3-1）

Behavioral essentials:

(1) Stand on the balances board with your feet apart.

(2) Keep your back straight, hold a dumbbell in each hand.

(3) Keep your arms straight and do lateral raise. (Fig.5-3-1)

图 5-3-1 平衡盘上侧平举

Fig.5-3-1 Flat lifting on the upper side of the balance plate

负荷强度：3 组，每组 12 次，每组间歇 15 秒。

Intensity: 3 sets in all, each set for 12 times,

then taking a 15-second break.

注意事项：

（1）腰、背部收紧。

（2）腰部挺直。

（3）手臂伸直。

Attentions:

(1) Tighten your waist and back.

(2) Keep your waist straight.

(3) Straighten your arms.

2. 平衡盘上马步前平举 A Flat Lift on Balance Board

锻炼部位：三角肌、腹直肌、肱四头肌、臀大肌。

Muscles exercised: Deltoid, rectus abdominis, brachial quadriceps, gluteus maximus.

动作要领：

（1）两脚开立与肩同宽，马步蹲于平衡盘上。

（2）背部挺直，两臂伸直各握一哑铃置于胸前。

（3）直臂前平举。（图 5-3-2）

Behavioral essentials:

(1) Your feet are shoulder-width apart, and squat on the balance board.

(2) Keep your back and arms straight,hold a dumbbell in each hand in front of the chest.

(3) Raise your arms straight in front of you. (Fig.5-3-2)

负荷强度：3 组，每组 12 次，每组间歇 15 秒。

Intensity: 3 sets in all, each set for 12 times, then taking a 15-second break.

图 5–3–2　平衡盘上马步前平举

Fig.5–3–2　A flat lift on balance board

注意事项：

（1）腰、背部收紧。

（2）两臂伸直，肩部打开。

（3）马步下蹲时大腿保持在水平面上。

Attentions:

(1) Tighten your waist and back.

(2) Keep your arms straight and your shoulders open.

(3) When you squat, keep your thighs parallel to the ground.

3. 平衡盘举哑铃上体侧屈 The Upper Body Lateral Flexion with Lifting Dumbbell on Balance Board

锻炼部位：前锯肌、腹横肌。

Muscles exercised: Serratus anterior, transversus abdominis.

动作要领：

（1）两脚开立与肩同宽，站于平衡盘上。

（2）背部挺直，一侧手叉腰。

（3）另一侧臂伸直上举哑铃。

（4）上举臂向体侧侧屈，两臂交替进行。（图 5-3-3）

Behavioral essentials:

(1) Your feet are shoulder-width apart, and stand on the balance boards.

(2) Keep your back straight and one hand on the waist.

(3) On the other side, lift the dumbbell and keep your arm straight up.

(4) The upper arm move sideways to do lateral flexion. Do it alternately. (Fig.5-3-3)

负荷强度：3 组，每组 12 次，每组间歇 15 秒。

Intensity: 3 sets in all, each set for 12 times, then taking a 15-second break.

注意事项：

（1）腰、腹部收紧。

（2）上举臂伸直。

Attention:

(1) Tighten your waist and abdomen.

(2) Straighten your upper arm.

图 5–3–3　平衡盘举哑铃上体侧屈

Fig.5–3–3　The upper body lateral flexion with lifting dumbbell on balance board

4. 弓步前腿站立平衡盘举哑铃蹲起 Dumbbell Lunge Squat with Front Leg on Balance Board

锻炼部位：股四头肌、三角肌、腹直肌。

Muscles exercised: Quadriceps femoris, deltoid, rectus abdominis.

动作要领：

（1）目视前方。

（2）前腿支撑于平衡盘上成前弓步。

（3）双手持哑铃下蹲。

（4）躯干保持正直。（图 5-3-4）

Behavioral essentials:

(1) Look ahead.

(2) Keep your front leg on the balance board and do lunge.

(3) Squat with dumbbells in both hands.

(4) Keep your torso upright. (Fig.5-3-4)

负荷强度：3 组，每组 12 次，每组间歇 15 秒。

Intensity: 3 sets in all, each set for 12 times, then taking a 15-second break.

注意事项：

（1）身体保持正直。

（2）下蹲时膝关节不能超过脚尖。

（3）身体不能左右摇摆。

Attention:

(1) Keep your body upright.

(2) Knee flexion can not exceed the tiptoe.

(3) Body can not swing.

图 5–3–4　弓步前腿站立平衡盘举哑铃蹲起

Fig.5–3–4　Dumbbell lunge squat with front leg on balance board

5. 平衡盘单腿弓步举杠铃蹲起 Barbell Lunge Squat with Front Leg on Balance Board

锻炼部位：股四头肌、腹直肌。

Muscles exercised: Quadriceps femoris, rectus abdominis.

动作要领：

（1）目视前方。

（2）前腿支撑于平衡盘上成前弓步。

（3）双手持杠铃下蹲。

（4）躯干保持正直。（图 5-3-5）

Behavioral essentials:

(1) Look ahead.

(2) Keep the front leg on the balance board and do lunge.

(3) Squat with a barbell in hands.

(4) Keep the torso upright. (Fig.5-3-5)

负荷强度：3 组，每组 12 次，每组间歇 15 秒。

Intensity: 3 sets in all, each set for 12 times, then taking a 15-second break.

图 5–3–5　平衡盘单腿弓步举杠铃蹲起

Fig.5–3–5　Barbell lunge squat with front leg on balance board

注意事项：

（1）身体保持正直。

（2）下蹲时膝关节不能超过脚尖。

（3）身体不能左右摇摆。

Attentions:

(1) Keep your body upright.

(2) Knee flexion can not exceed the tiptoes.

(3) Body can not swing.

6. 平衡盘站立负重蹲起 Weight-bearing Squat by Standing on Balance Board

锻炼部位：股四头肌、腹直肌、臀大肌。

Muscles exercised: Quadriceps femoris, rectus abdominis, gluteus maximus.

动作要领：

（1）两脚开立与肩同宽，站于平衡盘上。

（2）目视前方。

（3）双手持杠铃做马步下蹲动作。

（4）保持躯干直立。（图 5-3-6）

Behavioral essentials:

(1) The feet are shoulder-width apart, and stand on the balance boards.

(2) Look ahead.

(3) Squat holding a barbell in both hands.

(4) Keep the trunk upright. (Fig.5-3-6)

负荷强度：3 组，每组 12 次，每组间歇 15 秒。

Intensity: 3 sets in all, each set for 12 times, then taking a 15-second break.

注意事项：

（1）腰、腹、背部收紧。

（2）两臂伸直。

（3）下蹲时保持身体正直。

Attentions:

(1) Tighten your waist, abdomen and back.

(2) Keep your arms straight.

(3) Keep your body upright when you squat.

图 5–3–6　平衡盘站立负重蹲起

Fig .5–3–6　Weight–bearing squat by standing on balance board

7. 平衡盘侧弓步举杠铃蹲起 Barbell Lateral Lunge Squat on Balance Board

锻炼部位：股四头肌、腹直肌、臀大肌。

Muscles exercised: Quadriceps femoris, rectus abdominis, gluteus maximus.

动作要领：

（1）目视前方，站立成侧弓步。

（2）弓步弯曲腿支撑于平衡盘上。

（3）双手持杠铃做弓步下蹲动作。

（4）保持躯干直立。（图 5-3-7）

Behavioral essentials:

(1) Look ahead and do a side lateral lunge.

(2) The bending leg is on the balance board.

(3) Squat with holding a barbell in both hands.

(4) Keep the trunk upright. (Fig.5-3-7)

负荷强度：3 组，每组 12 次，每组间歇 15 秒。

Intensity: 3 sets in all, each set for 12 times, then taking a 15-second break.

注意事项：

（1）腰、腹、背部收紧。

（2）两臂伸直。

（3）动作缓慢进行。

（4）下蹲时保持身体正直。

Attentions:

(1) Tighten your waist, abdomen and back.

(2) Keep your arms straight.

(3) Move slowly.

(4) Keep your body upright when you squat.

图 5-3-7　平衡盘侧弓步举杠铃蹲起

Fig.5-3-7　Barbell lateral lunge squat on balance board

CHAPTER 6

第六章

核心力量测量与评价

Measurement and Evaluation of Core Strength

第一节 核心力量测量与评价简介

Section 1 Introduction of the Measurement and Evaluation of Core Strength

核心力量测试是评价核心稳定性、诊断核心专门性力量、发现弱链环节、制订训练计划、设计训练方法以及合理规划总体训练目标的有效途径。

Core strength test is an effective way to evaluate core stability, diagnose core specialized power, discover weak chains in the course of training, develop training plans of core strength, design training methods and rationally plan overall training goals.

通过试验的方法，测定大学生核心力量区域的生理情况优劣，测定与评价经过核心力量训练之后学生的锻炼效果。同时，利用核心力量练习评价量表，推动大学生自我评价与参与训练评价。

Through the test, the physiological condition of the core strength area of college students is determined and the exercise effect of the students after core strength training is measured and evaluated. At the same time, the core strength practice evaluation table can promote the self-evaluation and participate training evaluation of college students.

大学生“核心区力量训练＋评价”的体育课模式有别于专业训练，遵守简单、方便的原则，注重对学生耐力和灵敏度的培养，以提升学生身体的整体素质为最终目的，以教会学生如何锻炼身体，培养学生的运动兴趣为目标。能够丰富体育课教学体系，正确评价大学生肌肉状况与核心力量训练效果，激发大学生主动参与体育训练，有效改善当前大学生久坐、运动量不足造成的身体素质低下的状况，提高大学生运动能力，为终身体育打下坚实的基础，进而增强我国国民体质健康。可以说，核心区力量训练是增强学生体质最好的选择。

The "Core Strength Training & Evaluation Scale" physical education class mode of college students is different from the professional training for sports competition. It adheres to simplicity and convenience, and pays attention to the cultivation of students' endurance and sensitivity. It aims at teaching students how to exercise and cultivating students' interest in sports. It can enrich the physical education system; correctly evaluate the muscle condition and core strength training effect of college students; motivate college students to actively participate in physical training; effectively improve the current situation of low physical fitness caused by too much sitting and insufficient exercise; improve the sports ability of college student; lay a solid foundation for lifelong sports and improve the physical health of our people. It can be said that core strength training is the best choice to enhance students' physique.

核心力量练习评价量表（参考）如表 6–1–1 所示。

Core Strength Practice Evaluation Table（Reference）as shown in Table 6-1-1.

表 6-1-1　核心力量训练评价量表（参考）

序号	动作类型	训练类型	动作名称	测试要求	不及格	及格	一般	良好	优秀	备注
1	核心力量徒手训练篇	腹部与核心肌群组合训练	单腿两头起	测试指标：时间 / 个数；测试单位：s/ 个	A ≤ X < B	B ≤ X < C	C ≤ X < D	D ≤ X < E	E ≤ X < F	
2			倒蹬车	测试指标：时间 / 个数；测试单位：s/ 个	A ≤ X < B	B ≤ X < C	C ≤ X < D	D ≤ X < E	E ≤ X < F	
3			仰卧单车	测试指标：时间 / 个数；测试单位：s/ 个	A ≤ X < B	B ≤ X < C	C ≤ X < D	D ≤ X < E	E ≤ X < F	
4			简化俄罗斯转体	测试指标：时间 / 个数；测试单位：s/ 个	A ≤ X < B	B ≤ X < C	C ≤ X < D	D ≤ X < E	E ≤ X < F	
5			俯卧交替抬腿	测试指标：时间 / 个数；测试单位：s/ 个	A ≤ X < B	B ≤ X < C	C ≤ X < D	D ≤ X < E	E ≤ X < F	
6			俯卧提膝	测试指标：时间 / 个数；测试单位：s/ 个	A ≤ X < B	B ≤ X < C	C ≤ X < D	D ≤ X < E	E ≤ X < F	
7			V 字支撑转体	测试指标：时间 / 个数；测试单位：s/ 个	A ≤ X < B	B ≤ X < C	C ≤ X < D	D ≤ X < E	E ≤ X < F	
8			收腹举腿	测试指标：时间 / 个数；测试单位：s/ 个	A ≤ X < B	B ≤ X < C	C ≤ X < D	D ≤ X < E	E ≤ X < F	
9			摸膝	测试指标：时间 / 个数；测试单位：s/ 个	A ≤ X < B	B ≤ X < C	C ≤ X < D	D ≤ X < E	E ≤ X < F	
10			西西里卷腹	测试指标：时间 / 个数；测试单位：s/ 个	A ≤ X < B	B ≤ X < C	C ≤ X < D	D ≤ X < E	E ≤ X < F	
11			平板支撑	测试指标：时间 / 个数；测试单位：s/ 个	A ≤ X < B	B ≤ X < C	C ≤ X < D	D ≤ X < E	E ≤ X < F	

续表

序号	动作类型	训练类型	动作名称	测试要求	不及格	及格	一般	良好	优秀	备注
12	核心力量徒手训练篇	腹部与核心肌群组合训练	屈腿收腹	测试指标：时间 / 个数；测试单位：s/ 个	A ≤ X ＜ B	B ≤ X ＜ C	C ≤ X ＜ D	D ≤ X ＜ E	E ≤ X ＜ F	
13			反向卷腹	测试指标：时间 / 个数；测试单位：s/ 个	A ≤ X ＜ B	B ≤ X ＜ C	C ≤ X ＜ D	D ≤ X ＜ E	E ≤ X ＜ F	
14			十字交叉	测试指标：时间 / 个数；测试单位：s/ 个	A ≤ X ＜ B	B ≤ X ＜ C	C ≤ X ＜ D	D ≤ X ＜ E	E ≤ X ＜ F	
15			侧卧提臀	测试指标：时间 / 个数；测试单位：s/ 个	A ≤ X ＜ B	B ≤ X ＜ C	C ≤ X ＜ D	D ≤ X ＜ E	E ≤ X ＜ F	
16		背部与核心肌群组合训练	山羊挺身	测试指标：时间 / 个数；测试单位：s/ 个	A ≤ X ＜ B	B ≤ X ＜ C	C ≤ X ＜ D	D ≤ X ＜ E	E ≤ X ＜ F	
17			立式耸肩	测试指标：时间 / 个数；测试单位：s/ 个	A ≤ X ＜ B	B ≤ X ＜ C	C ≤ X ＜ D	D ≤ X ＜ E	E ≤ X ＜ F	
18			俯身平地两头起	测试指标：时间 / 个数；测试单位：s/ 个	A ≤ X ＜ B	B ≤ X ＜ C	C ≤ X ＜ D	D ≤ X ＜ E	E ≤ X ＜ F	
19			俯卧背腿	测试指标：时间 / 个数；测试单位：s/ 个	A ≤ X ＜ B	B ≤ X ＜ C	C ≤ X ＜ D	D ≤ X ＜ E	E ≤ X ＜ F	
20			猫式伸展	测试指标：时间 / 个数；测试单位：s/ 个	A ≤ X ＜ B	B ≤ X ＜ C	C ≤ X ＜ D	D ≤ X ＜ E	E ≤ X ＜ F	
21		腹部与背部组合训练	连续跳跃	测试指标：时间 / 个数；测试单位：s/ 个	A ≤ X ＜ B	B ≤ X ＜ C	C ≤ X ＜ D	D ≤ X ＜ E	E ≤ X ＜ F	
22			侧卧剪刀腿	测试指标：时间 / 个数；测试单位：s/ 个	A ≤ X ＜ B	B ≤ X ＜ C	C ≤ X ＜ D	D ≤ X ＜ E	E ≤ X ＜ F	

续表

序号	动作类型	训练类型	动作名称	测试要求	不及格	及格	一般	良好	优秀	备注
23	核心力量徒手训练篇	腹部与背部组合训练	站立提膝	测试指标：时间 / 个数；测试单位：s/ 个	A ≤ X < B	B ≤ X < C	C ≤ X < D	D ≤ X < E	E ≤ X < F	
24			陆地游泳	测试指标：时间 / 个数；测试单位：s/ 个	A ≤ X < B	B ≤ X < C	C ≤ X < D	D ≤ X < E	E ≤ X < F	
25			仰卧起坐	测试指标：时间 / 个数；测试单位：s/ 个	A ≤ X < B	B ≤ X < C	C ≤ X < D	D ≤ X < E	E ≤ X < F	
26			臂屈伸	测试指标：时间 / 个数；测试单位：s/ 个	A ≤ X < B	B ≤ X < C	C ≤ X < D	D ≤ X < E	E ≤ X < F	
27			臀桥	测试指标：时间 / 个数；测试单位：s/ 个	A ≤ X < B	B ≤ X < C	C ≤ X < D	D ≤ X < E	E ≤ X < F	
28	核心力量单一器械训练篇	平衡垫训练	平衡下蹲	测试指标：时间 / 个数；测试单位：s/ 个	A ≤ X < B	B ≤ X < C	C ≤ X < D	D ≤ X < E	E ≤ X < F	
29			综合平衡下蹲	测试指标：时间 / 个数；测试单位：s/ 个	A ≤ X < B	B ≤ X < C	C ≤ X < D	D ≤ X < E	E ≤ X < F	
30			平衡箭步蹲	测试指标：时间 / 个数；测试单位：s/ 个	A ≤ X < B	B ≤ X < C	C ≤ X < D	D ≤ X < E	E ≤ X < F	
31			飞鸟支撑	测试指标：时间 / 个数；测试单位：s/ 个	A ≤ X < B	B ≤ X < C	C ≤ X < D	D ≤ X < E	E ≤ X < F	
32			平衡控腹	测试指标：时间 / 个数；测试单位：s/ 个	A ≤ X < B	B ≤ X < C	C ≤ X < D	D ≤ X < E	E ≤ X < F	
33			平衡盘两头起	测试指标：时间 / 个数；测试单位：s/ 个	A ≤ X < B	B ≤ X < C	C ≤ X < D	D ≤ X < E	E ≤ X < F	

续表

序号	动作类型	训练类型	动作名称	测试要求	不及格	及格	一般	良好	优秀	备注
34	核心力量单一器械训练篇	平衡垫训练	仰卧交叉	测试指标：时间 / 个数；测试单位：s/ 个	A ≤ X < B	B ≤ X < C	C ≤ X < D	D ≤ X < E	E ≤ X < F	
35			腿夹平衡垫两头起	测试指标：时间 / 个数；测试单位：s/ 个	A ≤ X < B	B ≤ X < C	C ≤ X < D	D ≤ X < E	E ≤ X < F	
36			单腿收腹起	测试指标：时间 / 个数；测试单位：s/ 个	A ≤ X < B	B ≤ X < C	C ≤ X < D	D ≤ X < E	E ≤ X < F	
37			仰卧双腿顶髋	测试指标：时间 / 个数；测试单位：s/ 个	A ≤ X < B	B ≤ X < C	C ≤ X < D	D ≤ X < E	E ≤ X < F	
38			仰卧单腿顶髋	测试指标：时间 / 个数；测试单位：s/ 个	A ≤ X < B	B ≤ X < C	C ≤ X < D	D ≤ X < E	E ≤ X < F	
39			俯卧撑控肩	测试指标：时间 / 个数；测试单位：s/ 个	A ≤ X < B	B ≤ X < C	C ≤ X < D	D ≤ X < E	E ≤ X < F	
40			核心平板支撑	测试指标：时间 / 个数；测试单位：s/ 个	A ≤ X < B	B ≤ X < C	C ≤ X < D	D ≤ X < E	E ≤ X < F	
41			单臂平板支撑	测试指标：时间 / 个数；测试单位：s/ 个	A ≤ X < B	B ≤ X < C	C ≤ X < D	D ≤ X < E	E ≤ X < F	
42			侧卧肘支撑	测试指标：时间 / 个数；测试单位：s/ 个	A ≤ X < B	B ≤ X < C	C ≤ X < D	D ≤ X < E	E ≤ X < F	
43			侧卧肘支撑抬腿	测试指标：时间 / 个数；测试单位：s/ 个	A ≤ X < B	B ≤ X < C	C ≤ X < D	D ≤ X < E	E ≤ X < F	
44			侧卧肘支撑前后摆腿	测试指标：时间 / 个数；测试单位：s/ 个	A ≤ X < B	B ≤ X < C	C ≤ X < D	D ≤ X < E	E ≤ X < F	
45			侧卧肘支撑转体	测试指标：时间 / 个数；测试单位：s/ 个	A ≤ X < B	B ≤ X < C	C ≤ X < D	D ≤ X < E	E ≤ X < F	

续表

序号	动作类型	训练类型	动作名称	测试要求	不及格	及格	一般	良好	优秀	备注
46	核心力量单一器械训练篇	平衡垫训练	单腿平板支撑	测试指标：时间 / 个数；测试单位：s/ 个	A ≤ X < B	B ≤ X < C	C ≤ X < D	D ≤ X < E	E ≤ X < F	
47			俯卧背起	测试指标：时间 / 个数；测试单位：s/ 个	A ≤ X < B	B ≤ X < C	C ≤ X < D	D ≤ X < E	E ≤ X < F	
48			跪桥抬腿	测试指标：时间 / 个数；测试单位：s/ 个	A ≤ X < B	B ≤ X < C	C ≤ X < D	D ≤ X < E	E ≤ X < F	
49			跪桥单手单腿支撑	测试指标：时间 / 个数；测试单位：s/ 个	A ≤ X < B	B ≤ X < C	C ≤ X < D	D ≤ X < E	E ≤ X < F	
50		哑铃、杠铃训练	哑铃侧蹲	测试指标：时间 / 个数；测试单位：s/ 个	A ≤ X < B	B ≤ X < C	C ≤ X < D	D ≤ X < E	E ≤ X < F	
51			哑铃侧平举	测试指标：时间 / 个数；测试单位：s/ 个	A ≤ X < B	B ≤ X < C	C ≤ X < D	D ≤ X < E	E ≤ X < F	
52			哑铃卧推	测试指标：时间 / 个数；测试单位：s/ 个	A ≤ X < B	B ≤ X < C	C ≤ X < D	D ≤ X < E	E ≤ X < F	
53			哑铃臂前伸	测试指标：时间 / 个数；测试单位：s/ 个	A ≤ X < B	B ≤ X < C	C ≤ X < D	D ≤ X < E	E ≤ X < F	
54			哑铃硬拉	测试指标：时间 / 个数；测试单位：s/ 个	A ≤ X < B	B ≤ X < C	C ≤ X < D	D ≤ X < E	E ≤ X < F	
55			哑铃 8 字划圈	测试指标：时间 / 个数；测试单位：s/ 个	A ≤ X < B	B ≤ X < C	C ≤ X < D	D ≤ X < E	E ≤ X < F	
56			左腿哑铃箭步蹲	测试指标：时间 / 个数；测试单位：s/ 个	A ≤ X < B	B ≤ X < C	C ≤ X < D	D ≤ X < E	E ≤ X < F	
57			右腿哑铃箭步蹲	测试指标：时间 / 个数；测试单位：s/ 个	A ≤ X < B	B ≤ X < C	C ≤ X < D	D ≤ X < E	E ≤ X < F	

续表

序号	动作类型	训练类型	动作名称	测试要求	不及格	及格	一般	良好	优秀	备注
58	核心力量单一器械训练篇	哑铃、杠铃训练	上斜哑铃飞鸟	测试指标：时间 / 个数；测试单位：s/ 个	A ≤ X < B	B ≤ X < C	C ≤ X < D	D ≤ X < E	E ≤ X < F	
59			哑铃钻石卧推	测试指标：时间 / 个数；测试单位：s/ 个	A ≤ X < B	B ≤ X < C	C ≤ X < D	D ≤ X < E	E ≤ X < F	
60			哑铃反握划船	测试指标：时间 / 个数；测试单位：s/ 个	A ≤ X < B	B ≤ X < C	C ≤ X < D	D ≤ X < E	E ≤ X < F	
61			仰卧哑铃屈伸	测试指标：时间 / 个数；测试单位：s/ 个	A ≤ X < B	B ≤ X < C	C ≤ X < D	D ≤ X < E	E ≤ X < F	
62			哑铃坐姿推举	测试指标：时间 / 个数；测试单位：s/ 个	A ≤ X < B	B ≤ X < C	C ≤ X < D	D ≤ X < E	E ≤ X < F	
63			哑铃后撤	测试指标：时间 / 个数；测试单位：s/ 个	A ≤ X < B	B ≤ X < C	C ≤ X < D	D ≤ X < E	E ≤ X < F	
64			哑铃臀桥卧推	测试指标：时间 / 个数；测试单位：s/ 个	A ≤ X < B	B ≤ X < C	C ≤ X < D	D ≤ X < E	E ≤ X < F	
65			宽握哑铃划船	测试指标：时间 / 个数；测试单位：s/ 个	A ≤ X < B	B ≤ X < C	C ≤ X < D	D ≤ X < E	E ≤ X < F	
66			哑铃平地飞鸟	测试指标：时间 / 个数；测试单位：s/ 个	A ≤ X < B	B ≤ X < C	C ≤ X < D	D ≤ X < E	E ≤ X < F	
67			哑铃俄罗斯转体	测试指标：时间 / 个数；测试单位：s/ 个	A ≤ X < B	B ≤ X < C	C ≤ X < D	D ≤ X < E	E ≤ X < F	
68			哑铃单臂划船	测试指标：时间 / 个数；测试单位：s/ 个	A ≤ X < B	B ≤ X < C	C ≤ X < D	D ≤ X < E	E ≤ X < F	
69			杠铃颈前推举	测试指标：时间 / 个数；测试单位：s/ 个	A ≤ X < B	B ≤ X < C	C ≤ X < D	D ≤ X < E	E ≤ X < F	

续表

序号	动作类型	训练类型	动作名称	测试要求	不及格	及格	一般	良好	优秀	备注
70	核心力量单一器械训练篇	哑铃、杠铃训练	杠铃颈后推举	测试指标：时间 / 个数；测试单位：s/ 个	$A \leqslant X < B$	$B \leqslant X < C$	$C \leqslant X < D$	$D \leqslant X < E$	$E \leqslant X < F$	
71			仰卧杠铃臂屈伸	测试指标：时间 / 个数；测试单位：s/ 个	$A \leqslant X < B$	$B \leqslant X < C$	$C \leqslant X < D$	$D \leqslant X < E$	$E \leqslant X < F$	
72			窄握杠铃推举	测试指标：时间 / 个数；测试单位：s/ 个	$A \leqslant X < B$	$B \leqslant X < C$	$C \leqslant X < D$	$D \leqslant X < E$	$E \leqslant X < F$	
73			直立杠铃弯举	测试指标：时间 / 个数；测试单位：s/ 个	$A \leqslant X < B$	$B \leqslant X < C$	$C \leqslant X < D$	$D \leqslant X < E$	$E \leqslant X < F$	
74			杠铃俯身划船	测试指标：时间 / 个数；测试单位：s/ 个	$A \leqslant X < B$	$B \leqslant X < C$	$C \leqslant X < D$	$D \leqslant X < E$	$E \leqslant X < F$	
75			“T”杠俯身划船	测试指标：时间 / 个数；测试单位：s/ 个	$A \leqslant X < B$	$B \leqslant X < C$	$C \leqslant X < D$	$D \leqslant X < E$	$E \leqslant X < F$	
76			负重耸肩	测试指标：时间 / 个数；测试单位：s/ 个	$A \leqslant X < B$	$B \leqslant X < C$	$C \leqslant X < D$	$D \leqslant X < E$	$E \leqslant X < F$	
77			负重躬身	测试指标：时间 / 个数；测试单位：s/ 个	$A \leqslant X < B$	$B \leqslant X < C$	$C \leqslant X < D$	$D \leqslant X < E$	$E \leqslant X < F$	
78			屈腿硬拉	测试指标：时间 / 个数；测试单位：s/ 个	$A \leqslant X < B$	$B \leqslant X < C$	$C \leqslant X < D$	$D \leqslant X < E$	$E \leqslant X < F$	
79			史密斯卧推	测试指标：时间 / 个数；测试单位：s/ 个	$A \leqslant X < B$	$B \leqslant X < C$	$C \leqslant X < D$	$D \leqslant X < E$	$E \leqslant X < F$	
80			平板杠铃卧推	测试指标：时间 / 个数；测试单位：s/ 个	$A \leqslant X < B$	$B \leqslant X < C$	$C \leqslant X < D$	$D \leqslant X < E$	$E \leqslant X < F$	
81			上斜杠铃卧推	测试指标：时间 / 个数；测试单位：s/ 个	$A \leqslant X < B$	$B \leqslant X < C$	$C \leqslant X < D$	$D \leqslant X < E$	$E \leqslant X < F$	

续表

序号	动作类型	训练类型	动作名称	测试要求	不及格	及格	一般	良好	优秀	备注
82	核心力量单一器械训练篇	哑铃、杠铃训练	颈后深蹲	测试指标：时间 / 个数；测试单位：s/ 个	A ≤ X < B	B ≤ X < C	C ≤ X < D	D ≤ X < E	E ≤ X < F	
83			仰卧提臀	测试指标：时间 / 个数；测试单位：s/ 个	A ≤ X < B	B ≤ X < C	C ≤ X < D	D ≤ X < E	E ≤ X < F	
84			史密斯深蹲	测试指标：时间 / 个数；测试单位：s/ 个	A ≤ X < B	B ≤ X < C	C ≤ X < D	D ≤ X < E	E ≤ X < F	
85			箭步蹲杠铃	测试指标：时间 / 个数；测试单位：s/ 个	A ≤ X < B	B ≤ X < C	C ≤ X < D	D ≤ X < E	E ≤ X < F	
86			直腿硬拉	测试指标：时间 / 个数；测试单位：s/ 个	A ≤ X < B	B ≤ X < C	C ≤ X < D	D ≤ X < E	E ≤ X < F	
87		瑞士球训练	双腿支撑俯卧撑	测试指标：时间 / 个数；测试单位：s/ 个	A ≤ X < B	B ≤ X < C	C ≤ X < D	D ≤ X < E	E ≤ X < F	
88			双脚脚尖支撑俯卧撑	测试指标：时间 / 个数；测试单位：s/ 个	A ≤ X < B	B ≤ X < C	C ≤ X < D	D ≤ X < E	E ≤ X < F	
89			单腿支撑俯卧撑	测试指标：时间 / 个数；测试单位：s/ 个	A ≤ X < B	B ≤ X < C	C ≤ X < D	D ≤ X < E	E ≤ X < F	
90			双腿支撑爬行	测试指标：时间 / 个数；测试单位：s/ 个	A ≤ X < B	B ≤ X < C	C ≤ X < D	D ≤ X < E	E ≤ X < F	
91			单腿支撑爬行	测试指标：时间 / 个数；测试单位：s/ 个	A ≤ X < B	B ≤ X < C	C ≤ X < D	D ≤ X < E	E ≤ X < F	
92			双球支撑俯卧撑	测试指标：时间 / 个数；测试单位：s/ 个	A ≤ X < B	B ≤ X < C	C ≤ X < D	D ≤ X < E	E ≤ X < F	
93			双肘支撑外扩内收	测试指标：时间 / 个数；测试单位：s/ 个	A ≤ X < B	B ≤ X < C	C ≤ X < D	D ≤ X < E	E ≤ X < F	

续表

序号	动作类型	训练类型	动作名称	测试要求	不及格	及格	一般	良好	优秀	备注
94	核心力量单一器械训练篇	瑞士球训练	前后滚动双球	测试指标：时间 / 个数；测试单位：s/ 个	A ≤ X < B	B ≤ X < C	C ≤ X < D	D ≤ X < E	E ≤ X < F	
95			双腿搭球卷腹	测试指标：时间 / 个数；测试单位：s/ 个	A ≤ X < B	B ≤ X < C	C ≤ X < D	D ≤ X < E	E ≤ X < F	
96			仰卧屈膝夹球转髋	测试指标：时间 / 个数；测试单位：s/ 个	A ≤ X < B	B ≤ X < C	C ≤ X < D	D ≤ X < E	E ≤ X < F	
97			仰卧双腿夹球上摆	测试指标：时间 / 个数；测试单位：s/ 个	A ≤ X < B	B ≤ X < C	C ≤ X < D	D ≤ X < E	E ≤ X < F	
98			坐立仰卧起坐	测试指标：时间 / 个数；测试单位：s/ 个	A ≤ X < B	B ≤ X < C	C ≤ X < D	D ≤ X < E	E ≤ X < F	
99			抱头体侧屈	测试指标：时间 / 个数；测试单位：s/ 个	A ≤ X < B	B ≤ X < C	C ≤ X < D	D ≤ X < E	E ≤ X < F	
100			瑞士球屈腿内收	测试指标：时间 / 个数；测试单位：s/ 个	A ≤ X < B	B ≤ X < C	C ≤ X < D	D ≤ X < E	E ≤ X < F	
101			瑞士球屈膝内收	测试指标：时间 / 个数；测试单位：s/ 个	A ≤ X < B	B ≤ X < C	C ≤ X < D	D ≤ X < E	E ≤ X < F	
102			俯卧双腿支撑收腹	测试指标：时间 / 个数；测试单位：s/ 个	A ≤ X < B	B ≤ X < C	C ≤ X < D	D ≤ X < E	E ≤ X < F	
103			俯撑撞击弹回	测试指标：时间 / 个数；测试单位：s/ 个	A ≤ X < B	B ≤ X < C	C ≤ X < D	D ≤ X < E	E ≤ X < F	
104			仰卧持球直臂转体	测试指标：时间 / 个数；测试单位：s/ 个	A ≤ X < B	B ≤ X < C	C ≤ X < D	D ≤ X < E	E ≤ X < F	
105			仰卧支撑提臀	测试指标：时间 / 个数；测试单位：s/ 个	A ≤ X < B	B ≤ X < C	C ≤ X < D	D ≤ X < E	E ≤ X < F	

续表

序号	动作类型	训练类型	动作名称	测试要求	不及格	及格	一般	良好	优秀	备注
106	核心力量单一器械训练篇	瑞士球训练	倚球支撑蹲伸	测试指标：时间 / 个数；测试单位：s/ 个	A ≤ X < B	B ≤ X < C	C ≤ X < D	D ≤ X < E	E ≤ X < F	
107			瑞士球仰卧起坐	测试指标：时间 / 个数；测试单位：s/ 个	A ≤ X < B	B ≤ X < C	C ≤ X < D	D ≤ X < E	E ≤ X < F	
108			瑞士球俯卧背起	测试指标：时间 / 个数；测试单位：s/ 个	A ≤ X < B	B ≤ X < C	C ≤ X < D	D ≤ X < E	E ≤ X < F	
109			瑞士球俯拜	测试指标：时间 / 个数；测试单位：s/ 个	A ≤ X < B	B ≤ X < C	C ≤ X < D	D ≤ X < E	E ≤ X < F	
110			俯撑前后滑动	测试指标：时间 / 个数；测试单位：s/ 个	A ≤ X < B	B ≤ X < C	C ≤ X < D	D ≤ X < E	E ≤ X < F	
111			俯撑前滚屈肘	测试指标：时间 / 个数；测试单位：s/ 个	A ≤ X < B	B ≤ X < C	C ≤ X < D	D ≤ X < E	E ≤ X < F	
112			四点支撑平衡练习	测试指标：时间 / 个数；测试单位：s/ 个	A ≤ X < B	B ≤ X < C	C ≤ X < D	D ≤ X < E	E ≤ X < F	
113	核心力量复合器械训练篇	瑞士球组合训练	瑞士球支撑收腹	测试指标：时间 / 个数；测试单位：s/ 个	A ≤ X < B	B ≤ X < C	C ≤ X < D	D ≤ X < E	E ≤ X < F	
114			瑞士球跪姿收腹	测试指标：时间 / 个数；测试单位：s/ 个	A ≤ X < B	B ≤ X < C	C ≤ X < D	D ≤ X < E	E ≤ X < F	
115			瑞士球反向卷腹	测试指标：时间 / 个数；测试单位：s/ 个	A ≤ X < B	B ≤ X < C	C ≤ X < D	D ≤ X < E	E ≤ X < F	
116			瑞士球转体卷腹	测试指标：时间 / 个数；测试单位：s/ 个	A ≤ X < B	B ≤ X < C	C ≤ X < D	D ≤ X < E	E ≤ X < F	
117			瑞士球仰卧递球	测试指标：时间 / 个数；测试单位：s/ 个	A ≤ X < B	B ≤ X < C	C ≤ X < D	D ≤ X < E	E ≤ X < F	

续表

序号	动作类型	训练类型	动作名称	测试要求	不及格	及格	一般	良好	优秀	备注
118	核心力量复合器械训练篇	瑞士球组合训练	瑞士球弓步哑铃蹲起	测试指标：时间 / 个数；测试单位：s/ 个	A ≤ X < B	B ≤ X < C	C ≤ X < D	D ≤ X < E	E ≤ X < F	
119			仰卧瑞士球哑铃飞	测试指标：时间 / 个数；测试单位：s/ 个	A ≤ X < B	B ≤ X < C	C ≤ X < D	D ≤ X < E	E ≤ X < F	
120			瑞士球上负重体屈伸	测试指标：时间 / 个数；测试单位：s/ 个	A ≤ X < B	B ≤ X < C	C ≤ X < D	D ≤ X < E	E ≤ X < F	
121			瑞士球上负重转体	测试指标：时间 / 个数；测试单位：s/ 个	A ≤ X < B	B ≤ X < C	C ≤ X < D	D ≤ X < E	E ≤ X < F	
122			瑞士球上卧推	测试指标：时间 / 个数；测试单位：s/ 个	A ≤ X < B	B ≤ X < C	C ≤ X < D	D ≤ X < E	E ≤ X < F	
123			瑞士球弓步负重蹲起	测试指标：时间 / 个数；测试单位：s/ 个	A ≤ X < B	B ≤ X < C	C ≤ X < D	D ≤ X < E	E ≤ X < F	
124			瑞士球俯卧后抬腿	测试指标：时间 / 个数；测试单位：s/ 个	A ≤ X < B	B ≤ X < C	C ≤ X < D	D ≤ X < E	E ≤ X < F	
125			肘撑瑞士球后踢腿	测试指标：时间 / 个数；测试单位：s/ 个	A ≤ X < B	B ≤ X < C	C ≤ X < D	D ≤ X < E	E ≤ X < F	
126			肘撑瑞士球斜后踢腿	测试指标：时间 / 个数；测试单位：s/ 个	A ≤ X < B	B ≤ X < C	C ≤ X < D	D ≤ X < E	E ≤ X < F	
127			仰卧瑞士球向上踢腿	测试指标：时间 / 个数；测试单位：s/ 个	A ≤ X < B	B ≤ X < C	C ≤ X < D	D ≤ X < E	E ≤ X < F	
128		弹力带组合训练	平衡盘弓步绳索划船	测试指标：时间 / 个数；测试单位：s/ 个	A ≤ X < B	B ≤ X < C	C ≤ X < D	D ≤ X < E	E ≤ X < F	
129			弹力带平衡盘身体侧拉	测试指标：时间 / 个数；测试单位：s/ 个	A ≤ X < B	B ≤ X < C	C ≤ X < D	D ≤ X < E	E ≤ X < F	

续表

序号	动作类型	训练类型	动作名称	测试要求	不及格	及格	一般	良好	优秀	备注
130	核心力量复合器械训练篇	弹力带组合训练	平衡盘单手侧支撑拉弹力带	测试指标：时间 / 个数；测试单位：s/ 个	A ≤ X < B	B ≤ X < C	C ≤ X < D	D ≤ X < E	E ≤ X < F	
131			瑞士球坐姿斜拉	测试指标：时间 / 个数；测试单位：s/ 个	A ≤ X < B	B ≤ X < C	C ≤ X < D	D ≤ X < E	E ≤ X < F	
132			瑞士球坐姿单臂后拉	测试指标：时间 / 个数；测试单位：s/ 个	A ≤ X < B	B ≤ X < C	C ≤ X < D	D ≤ X < E	E ≤ X < F	
133			瑞士球 + 弹力带转体侧拉	测试指标：时间 / 个数；测试单位：s/ 个	A ≤ X < B	B ≤ X < C	C ≤ X < D	D ≤ X < E	E ≤ X < F	
134		平衡盘组合训练	平衡盘上侧平举	测试指标：时间 / 个数；测试单位：s/ 个	A ≤ X < B	B ≤ X < C	C ≤ X < D	D ≤ X < E	E ≤ X < F	
135			平衡盘上马步前平举	测试指标：时间 / 个数；测试单位：s/ 个	A ≤ X < B	B ≤ X < C	C ≤ X < D	D ≤ X < E	E ≤ X < F	
136			平衡盘举哑铃上体侧屈	测试指标：时间 / 个数；测试单位：s/ 个	A ≤ X < B	B ≤ X < C	C ≤ X < D	D ≤ X < E	E ≤ X < F	
137			弓步前腿站立平衡盘举哑铃蹲起	测试指标：时间 / 个数；测试单位：s/ 个	A ≤ X < B	B ≤ X < C	C ≤ X < D	D ≤ X < E	E ≤ X < F	
138			平衡盘单腿弓步举杠铃蹲起	测试指标：时间 / 个数；测试单位：s/ 个	A ≤ X < B	B ≤ X < C	C ≤ X < D	D ≤ X < E	E ≤ X < F	
139			平衡盘站立负重蹲起	测试指标：时间 / 个数；测试单位：s/ 个	A ≤ X < B	B ≤ X < C	C ≤ X < D	D ≤ X < E	E ≤ X < F	

续表

序号	动作类型	训练类型	动作名称	测试要求	不及格	及格	一般	良好	优秀	备注
140	核心力量复合器械训练篇	平衡盘组合训练	平衡盘侧弓步举杠铃蹲起	测试指标：时间 / 个数；测试单位：s/ 个	$A \leqslant X < B$	$B \leqslant X < C$	$C \leqslant X < D$	$D \leqslant X < E$	$E \leqslant X < F$	

第二节　核心力量测量与评价实施方法

Section 2　Implementation Methods of Core Strength Measurement and Evaluation

1. 核心稳定性测试 Core Stability Test

（1）测试要求。

(1) Testing Requirements.

测试者呈俯卧姿势，以肘部及脚尖为支点，将身体撑起，骨盆处于中立位，头、肩、髋、膝、踝成一条直线，肘关节屈成 90°，前臂平行与肩同宽，然后依次按时间完成表 6–2–1 中所列出的动作。

Let the testee be in a prone position, use the elbows and tiptoes hold the body up and the pelvis is in a neutral position. The head, shoulders, hips, knees, and ankles are in a straight line, the elbows are bent at 90° , and the forearms are parallel and shoulder-width apart. Then make the actions listed in Table 6-2-1 one by one.

表 6–2–1　八级俯桥测试评分参考标准

动作名称	得分等级	标准动作时间(s)	动作要求	动作等级	动作负荷
俯桥 1	较差	30	起始姿势 30	基础动作	低
俯桥 3	一般	45	抬起右臂 15 秒，还原	初级动作	中低
俯桥 5	一般	60	抬起左臂 15 秒，还原	初级动作	中低
俯桥 6	中等	75	抬起右腿 15 秒，还原	中级动作	中等
俯桥 10	中等	90	抬起左腿 15 秒，还原	中级动作	中等
俯桥 15	良好	105	抬起右臂及左腿 15 秒，还原	高级动作	高
俯桥 25	良好	120	抬起左臂及右腿 15 秒，还原	高级动作	高
俯桥 35	优秀	150	起始姿势维持 30 秒，还原	基础动作	较高

Table 6–2–1　Scoring Reference Standards for the Eight–Level Plank Test

Exercise name	Score level	Standard duration (s)	Movement requirement	Movement classification	Exercise load
Plank 1	Poor	30	Maintain the starting position 30s	Fundamental movement	Low

Continued table

Exercise Name	Score Level	Standard duration (s)	Movement Requirement	Movement Classification	Exercise Load
Plank 3	Average	45	Lift the right arm for 15s, then return	Beginner movement	Low–Medium
Plank 5	Average	60	Lift the left arm for 15s, then return	Beginner movement	Low–Medium
Plank 6	Medium	75	Lift the right leg for 15s, Restore	Intermediate movement	Medium
Plank 10	Medium	90	Lift the left leg for 15s, then return	Intermediate movement	Medium
Plank 15	Good	105	Lift the right arm and left leg 15s, then return	Advanced movement	High
Plank 25	Good	120	Lift the left arm and right leg 15s, then return	Advanced movement	High
Plank 35	Excellent	150	Maintain the starting position for 30, then return	Fundamental movement	Relative High

整体动作应做到：①侧视：耳、肩、髋、膝、踝始终保持一条直线；②俯视：身体两侧对称，不向一侧倾斜或弯曲（髋关节处）；③腰背平直，顶髋收腹，保持髋部和支撑腿的稳定。

The overall movement should be: ① side-looking: keep ears, shoulders, hips, knees, and ankles always maintain a straight line; ② top view: the body should be symmetrical on both sides, not inclined or bent to any side（hip joint）; ③ keep the waist and back straight, against hips and hold your stomach in, the hips and the support legs are kept stable.

（2）测试方法。

(2) Testing Methods.

第 1 级：以肘部及脚尖为支点，将身体撑起，保持 30 秒，要求身体保持中立，耳、肩、髋、膝、踝始终保持在一条直线上。

Level 1: Support the body with elbows and tiptoes as the support point for 30s, keep the body in a neutral position. The ears, shoulders, hips, knees and ankles are always in a straight line.

第 2 级：抬起右臂，要求直臂抬高，置于耳后，保持 15 秒。

Level 2: Raise the right arm straight, place the arm behind the ear and hold for 15s.

第 3 级：右臂收回，抬起左臂，要求直臂抬高，置于耳后，保持 15 秒。

Level 3: Pull back the right arm and raise the left arm straight, place the left arm behind the ear and hold for 15s.

第 4 级：收回左臂，抬起右腿，要求直腿抬高，勾住脚尖，保持 15 秒。

Level 4: Withdraw the left arm, lift right leg straight, hook the tiptoe and maintain 15s.

第 5 级：收回右腿，抬起左腿，要求直腿抬高，勾住脚尖，保持 15 秒。

Level 5: Retract right leg, lift left leg straight, hook the toe and maintain 15s.

第 6 级：抬起右臂和左腿，要求右臂直臂抬高，置于耳后；左腿直腿抬高，勾住脚尖；保持 15 秒。

Level 6: Lift right arm and left leg, keep right arm straight raised, put it behind ear and keep left leg straight raised, hook the toe and hold for 15s.

第 7 级：收回右臂和左腿，抬起左臂和右腿，要求左臂直臂抬高，置于耳后；右腿直腿抬高，勾住脚尖；保持 15 秒。

Level 7: Retract right arm and left leg, lift left arm and right leg, keep left arm straight raised, put it behind ear and keep right leg straight raised, hook the tiptoe and maintain 15s.

第 8 级：回到第 1 级的姿势，保持 1 分钟。

Level 8: Return to the action at level 1 and hold for 1 minute.

（3）评分标准。

(3) Scoring Criteria.

根据测试者能够维持标准身体姿势（身体成一条直线，骨盆处于中立位）的时间，对照表格中的时间标准进行评分，测试中允许测试者有轻微偏差，但是如果骨盆离开中立位置（髋抬起或腰部下沉）或身体任何部分接触地面，计时应立即结束。

Rating testees based on the time they are able to maintain the standard body posture (the body is in a straight line and the pelvis is in a neutral position) and compare with the time in the table. The test allow the testee to have a slight deviation, but if the pelvis leaves the neutral position (hip lifted or the waist sinks) or any part of the body touches the ground, the counting should be ended immediately.

在测试过程中，如果运动员的技术动作不能达到规范要求，则评定为上一级水准，如在第 5 级的测试中不能达到升级标准的动作要求，并经提示后仍无法达到要求，则评定该运动员的成绩为上第 4 级水平。

In the process of testing, if the technical action of the athlete cannot meet the criterion, he is assessed at the former level. For example, if athlete's action cannot meet the requirement in the fifth level, and he still cannot meet the requirement after the prompt, then the athlete is at the fourth level.

2. 徒手动力性测试 Freehand Dynamic Testing

核心力量的动力性测试主要测试核心肌群的快速收缩力量和力量耐力水平，主要测试动作有仰卧两头起、侧卧两头起、跪姿俯卧挺身、站姿推拉滚轮、悬吊俯卧撑、站立支撑高抬腿等。

The dynamic tests of core strength mainly test the rapid contraction strength and strength endurance level of the core muscle group. The main test actions include v-up, lie on the side and v-up, hyperextensions in kneeling position, standing push-pull roller, suspension push-ups, standing support high leg lifts, etc.

3. 核心力量负重测试 The Load Test of Core Strength

核心力量的负重测试主要测试核心肌群的收缩力量、核心稳定性及整体协调控制能力，测试动作主要有单腿支撑持球转体侧摆、站立持球下蹲（或抓举杠铃）、负重下蹲、前抛实心球、后抛实心球和侧抛实心球等。

The load test of core strength mainly test the contraction strength, core stability and overall coordination control ability of the core muscle groups. The test actions mainly include holding a ball twist and lateral run-out with one leg, squat holding a ball（or grabbing the barbell）, squat with weight, forward throwing a solid ball, back throwing a solid ball，side throwing a solid ball, etc.